IT Service Management for Small IT Teams

IT Service Management for Small IT Teams

Adam Poppleton and Ken Holmes

First published in the UK in 2011
by
BSI
389 Chiswick High Road
London W4 4AL

© British Standards Institution 2011

All rights reserved. Except as permitted under the Copyright, Designs and Patents Act 1988, no part of this publication may be reproduced, stored in a retrieval system or transmitted in any form or by any means, electronic, photocopying, recording or otherwise, without prior permission in writing from the publisher.

Whilst every care has been taken in developing and compiling this publication, BSI accepts no liability for any loss or damage caused, arising directly or indirectly in connection with reliance on its contents except that such liability may not be excluded in law.

Whilst every effort has been made to trace all copyright holders, anyone claiming copyright should get in touch with the BSI at the above address.

BSI has no responsibility for the persistence or accuracy of URLs for external or third-party websites referred to in this book, and does not guarantee that any content on such websites is, or will remain, accurate or appropriate.

The right of Adam Poppleton and Ken Holmes to be identified as the authors of this Work has been asserted by them in accordance with sections 77 and 78 of the Copyright, Designs and Patents Act 1988.

Typeset in Great Britain by Letterpart Limited – letterpart.com

Printed in Great Britain by Berforts Group, www.berforts.co.uk

British Library Cataloguing in Publication Data

A catalogue record for this book is available from the British Library

ISBN 978 0 580 74254 5

Contents

Acknowledgements	vii
Sources	viii
Dedications	ix
Preface	x
How to use this book	xii

1 Introduction — 1
The Vision — 3

2 The IT service management landscape — 6
Overview — 6
A bit of history — 8
Associated concepts, models and tools — 9
Decisions, decisions … — 11

3 Planning for IT service management — 13
The gap analysis — 13
Gaining management commitment — 19
The people aspects — 29

4 Project initiation — 39

5 Implementing IT service management — 42
Governance – the overall management system — 42
The main points so far — 49
Resolution processes — 50
Control processes — 68
Relationship processes — 84
Service delivery processes — 94
Design and transition of new or changed services — 138

6 The continual service improvement cycle — 141
Continual improvement in ISO/IEC 20000 – the Deming Cycle — 141
Continual improvement in ITIL — 142
Six Sigma and continual improvement — 143
Implementing continual improvement — 144

7 ISO/IEC 20000 – to certify or not to certify — 146
The certification process — 146

Pros 148
Cons 148

8 Tools 151
Evaluating ITSM software tools 151
Service desk tools 152
Configuration and release management tools 154
Event monitoring tools 155
Performance and capacity planning tools 155
Information security management tools 156

9 Case studies 158

10 Additional processes and concepts relevant to IT service management 162
Additional processes 162
Additional concepts 165

Appendix A Templates 171
A.1 Gap analysis checklist 171
A.2 Risk assessment 172
A.3 Supplier catalogue 176
A.4 Service catalogue 177
A.5 Service improvement log 180
A.6 Major Incident Report 181
A.7 Service introduction checklist 182
A.8 - IT Skills Questionnaire example 186

Appendix B References and useful sources of information 187

Acknowledgements

The authors would like to thank the following people for their help in the writing of this book:

- Ian Tinsley, IS Manager, Accord Group
- Mike Russell, Service Delivery Manager, Serco
- Richard Griffiths, User Support Team Leader, Sandwell Homes
- Julia Helmsley, Commissioning Editor, BSI
- Bridget Kenyon, Head of Consultancy, Thales e-security
- Steve Ingall, Head of Consultancy, iCore Ltd
- Jerry Bradley, Head of IS, GDF Suez E&P
- Jack Robertson-Worsfold, IT Service Manager, BSI

Sources

All of the templates in Appendix A have been taken from www.iso20000templates.com.

Dedications

Ken Holmes – To my fiancée Victoria and my children Katie, Daniel, Chloe and Harry; love you always. Thanks to my Mum and Dad for always being there and to my Grandfather Leslie for leading the way in the book-writing department.

Adam Poppleton – To my wife Raylene and my wonderful children, Cole and Grace.

Preface

Dave reached the office shortly after 9.00 a.m. Bleary-eyed through having been up most of the night trying to resolve an issue with a server that turned out to have no maintenance contract and no backups, he sat down heavily at his desk, the resulting gust of wind scattering the various post-it notes that had been left there, informing him of things that needed to be done, things that weren't working and people to call so they could tell him that things weren't working and needed to be done.

He looked across the crowded office to the help desk, where a number of earnest-looking and very busy 20-somethings sat, frantically taking call after call whilst their harassed supervisor pleaded over the general hullaballoo, "Did anyone change anything last night? Anything? Anyone?"

A stack of new PCs engulfed the desk next to him, the latest in a long line of deliveries intended for hurried installation by an overstretched team of desk-side engineers. 'Maybe we should have planned a bit better before we installed the latest version of Office on everyone's machine three months ago', he reflected. The resulting flood of slow-PC complaints had kept the first-line, second-line and procurement teams busy ever since.

User service had suffered heavily as a result of the need to divert resources to the installations and Dave glanced down the ever-increasing list of overdue calls and sighed. 'It's probably a good job we never meet with user management', he thought. 'And lucky we don't have an SLA they can hang us by too'.

Dave sat back in his chair and took a deep breath. 'Another fun day at the office', he whispered wearily.

Of course, things may not be as bad as this within your company. The fact is that many small IT teams get by pretty well a lot of the time without having any formal IT service management in place. They deliver the required projects on time and are generally well thought of by the people they support. So what's all the fuss about? What is wrong with the way we do things now?

Well, one of the issues is that the current level of service usually comes at a price; in terms of staff effort and goodwill; in terms of cost and in terms of consistency. The service is good despite the lack of proactivity, not because of it. It is common to find that an IT team that is not using formal processes is harassed, fed up and making more use of temporary staff than may be necessary. There is often general agreement amongst the team that the same mistakes are being made time and time again, with no one taking ownership of fixing them once and for all. This leads to a lot of frustration that may be reflected in higher than average staff turnover or absence and world-weary negative attitudes.

Communication within the team and between teams is often poor, giving rise to mistrust and suspicion over the causes of problems and accusations that one team or individual has to constantly 'clean up' after another. Reactivity is king, often driven by users who give very little notice of requests such as office moves or new starters, partly (but often not completely) because they have never been told what notice is actually required or what their request involves.

The services delivered are those that the IT team assume the users want, in the way that they assume the users want them. Meanwhile, the users may have local workarounds to cope with the perceived inadequacies of IT, but no one has the time to sit down and talk about how they might be changed. Major incidents such as systems failing or sites being down can be an almost daily occurrence, with the same actions being taken to resolve them every time, often without a clear idea of why – 'it just works ...'

In a small team, the 'techie' can wield a disproportionate amount of control and often lives by the mantra that 'knowledge is power', declining to communicate or document unless forced to do so. Testing is often thought unnecessary because, he declares, 'I know what I'm doing', and the big-bang approach is the standard implementation method for the same reason, with sometimes catastrophic results.

A reactive IT team is constantly surprised, whether it's by a server disk filling up or an office closing down. It may still deliver good service, but it's often by the skin of its teeth every time. But one of the best ways to tell whether implementing good practice will help you as an IT team is to talk to other teams that have already done it. Ask them whether they would go back to doing things the way they used to and we are confident that you will not find a single one that would. OK, they may admit that sometimes they reminisce about the days when they could just go ahead and change something or fix an issue without logging it, but would they abandon the control and stability they have experienced since they started doing it? We think not.

How to use this book

You just turn the pages, right? Well, yes, but we want you to get much more out of this book than just a theoretical appreciation of what IT service management is about. We want you to be able to take the ideas set out in these pages and really apply them to your small IT team. We know it's not easy; we know there are a lot of different areas covered, and we also know you're busy.

That's why we have tried to summarize the various approaches and sources of information about IT service management in short, hopefully easy-to-read chapters, ending with a concise summary and some pointers as to what to do next to move things forward in your organization. It's a big subject and inevitably there are some things we have left out either because we don't think they will be that useful to you or because they are more advanced concepts inappropriate for an introductory book such as this. You should also be aware that there are different ways of looking at some of the concepts of IT service management and in some areas the industry experts disagree with each other; we have tried to tread a middle ground based on our experience and put usefulness to a small IT team first in deciding what to cover.

We have also ordered the chapters in what we believe to be a logical sequence for someone attempting to implement the ideas as they go along. So we start with some typical reasons why organizations like yours make use of good practice and then go on to how to create a business case to convince your senior management that it is a good idea, before planning a service improvement project in detail.

But let us also point out that there is an alternative approach that the book will also support. Many organizations that have used these concepts never created a business case, did not secure any extra funding nor did they plan it as a project. They just took the ideas and started to apply them in small ways in the day-to-day management of their services. No grand plan, just improvement little by little. If things get busy they have a break from introducing improvements and when it's a bit quieter they spend more time on them. So this does not have to be a big deal within your team with pressured deadlines and high management expectations. Just start to do things differently, gradually.

Although we set out as full a list as we can of the current frameworks, standards and methods prevailing in IT service management at the

How to use this book

current time, we would freely admit that most of our experience (and therefore our advice) is based on ITIL (IT Infrastructure Library) Versions 2 and 3 and the ISO/IEC 20000 standard. This obviously has an effect on the structure of the book and the terminology used. Overall, however, the basic principles across ITIL, ISO/IEC 20000, COBIT, Six Sigma etc. are broadly similar and we have tried to concentrate on making the main ideas clear rather than pushing a particular way of doing things.

So, as you turn the pages, we hope each one will start to seed at least one idea of how you can make your life, that of your team and the delivery of IT services into your organization, better.

1 Introduction

The effective delivery of IT services plays an essential part in the survival and growth of a small organization through to maturity, especially in this internet-centric age. Many rely upon the internet to sell their products and reach customers so computer downtime will have a direct effect upon sales and therefore profitability. In tough economic conditions, stable IT services can be the difference between staying in business and going under.

It is tempting to think that IT service management good practice generally applies to larger organizations with seemingly limitless resources and global reputations to protect, but this is not necessarily the case. Smaller organizations have just as much to gain from the application of the ideas embedded in such frameworks, precisely because they don't have limitless resources. Good practice is all about getting the most from the resources you have and, if your team is small, this makes it even more relevant to you as an organization. Unfortunately many of the good practice guides that exist have to cater to multiple audiences and it is often the larger organizations that can afford to provide contributors to such work. The sheer complexity of IT service management within global organizations with hundreds of applications and thousands of users means that the management of their IT services becomes difficult by nature and this is inevitably reflected in the literature. But the principles that are established within such large companies often tend to scale down quite well and, as a small IT team, you are in a good position to benefit from the hard lessons that have cost the big players many millions and many years to learn.

But what do we mean by 'small IT team'? This is a question we have wrestled with to try to provide a reasonable answer. There are various definitions of 'small organization' in use within the UK, Europe, USA, Australia and Asia, using different criteria such as number of employees, turnover and value of assets, and varying also by the particular industry in question. Even where the same criteria are used, often the numbers are different, making a single definition difficult. If we then expand this to the definition of a small IT team specifically it becomes even more awkward, particularly if we take into account the effect of outsourcing, where sometimes significant IT operations are controlled by a small core team of in-house IT staff. Obviously the use of external suppliers is often essential so there will be some element of outsourcing typically present in most IT teams, but if the majority of IT support within your organization is carried out by third parties we would suggest that a book of this type is probably less appropriate and one on contract management would be more suitable.

However, we believe we owe it to you as the reader of this book to give the best indication we can of the size of team it is aimed at so that you can decide for yourself whether it is relevant to you. So, as a 'gut feel' indication, we would see the target IT team as consisting of around 25 or fewer staff, with a significant part of their IT support activities carried out in-house. Some people at whom this book is aimed would probably consider 25 to be a 'large' IT team and it is really all about perception; we have certainly implemented the ideas set out in these pages in an IT team of four, and believe they would still apply to a team of one.

Now that hopefully we have cleared that up, there are a number of distinct advantages to being small when implementing IT service management. These include:

- *Communication lines are shortened* – a small team, particularly one based at a single site, will tend to talk to each other on a frequent basis, and when new ideas need to be passed on this is usually a straightforward process.
- *Decisions can be made more quickly* – because there are fewer people involved in making them, decisions on approach, detail, timing etc. will tend to be made more quickly, thus allowing more to be achieved in the time available.
- *Training is delivered faster* – providing training to a small team is a faster process than if many sessions need to be organized, although the need to keep the service running must obviously be considered paramount.
- *Staff are often more flexible* – as staff in a small team tend to be multi-skilled there is often more willingness to learn new skills and perform several roles within the IT service management area.
- *Integration of processes can be easier if there are fewer process owners* – for example, where the owner of the incident, problem and change processes are the same person, integration can be achieved more effectively as potential conflict and the need for group co-ordination is reduced.

All of these factors can mean that the implementation timescale for new IT service management processes in a small IT team can be significantly shorter than that for a larger organization, and the benefits of following good practice can be felt more quickly. This means that users and IT staff can reap the rewards of better service in a time frame that most large organizations could only dream of.

It also helps to address a number of issues often faced by a typical small IT team including:

- *Depth of knowledge* – trying to ensure that IT staff have a reasonable depth as well as breadth of knowledge about the services they support. We will provide you with a method of assessing skills requirements and developing staff competencies in order to meet them.
- *Reliance on external suppliers* – small IT teams often have to rely upon the service provided by external support organizations, such as software suppliers and technical consultants. The supplier management process ensures that such relationships are based on a clear understanding of the levels of service provided and requires that delivery against them is measured and reviewed regularly, thus improving their effectiveness.
- *Workload peaks and troughs* – the varying volume of incidents, changes and projects demanded by the business can sometimes swamp a small IT team, leading to a reduction in the service delivered. IT service management provides ways of reducing incidents through problem management, managing changes more effectively and setting the expectations of the customer appropriately through regular meetings to discuss service and upcoming projects.
- *Impact of staff turnover, holidays and sickness* – due to the complexity of the various roles fulfilled by each member of the team, the loss of one member of staff can have a more serious effect on the service than in a larger organization where several people perform the same role. Often, the implementation of good practice has been shown to improve the morale of the IT team, that may help to reduce staff turnover. The emphasis on process and knowledge capture also means that a replacement can get up to speed more quickly.
- *Pressure on budgets* – the smaller IT team usually has less money to spend than its large company equivalent. The effective application of good practice helps to get the most out of existing staff, reducing the need to supplement resources with external contractors. Through the IT finance and supplier management processes it also helps to ensure that opportunities for cost saving are highlighted and provides the measurement data to be able to balance service levels and cost.

The Vision

So IT service management good practice can help a small IT team in all of the areas that have just been listed. But if we had to summarize the real contribution that it can potentially make to your team's standing in your organization, it would be using Figure 1.

1 Introduction

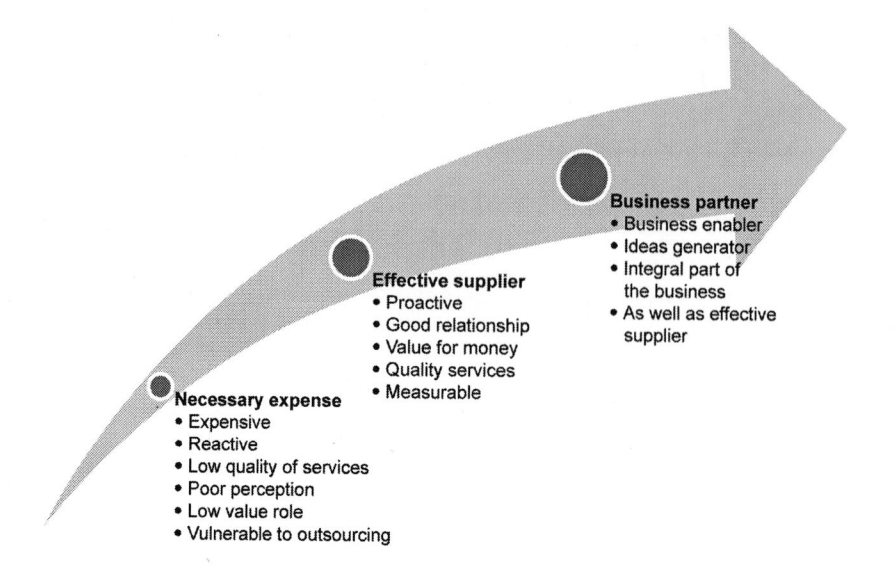

Necessary expense
- Expensive
- Reactive
- Low quality of services
- Poor perception
- Low value role
- Vulnerable to outsourcing

Effective supplier
- Proactive
- Good relationship
- Value for money
- Quality services
- Measurable

Business partner
- Business enabler
- Ideas generator
- Integral part of the business
- As well as effective supplier

Figure 1 – The Vision

All too many small IT teams are viewed by their parent organization as an expense that they would rather not have. Senior management realize that IT is a necessary part of a modern business but have little understanding of or contact with the IT department on a daily basis. It is perceived as a utility offering little business value and the IT Manager is rarely invited to senior management team meetings. Sometimes this view is taken to its logical conclusion and IT is outsourced to a third party. Now, situations vary and we are not saying for a moment that every small IT department is like this, and we hope yours isn't. The point is that the IT service management processes and techniques set out in this book will help you to further distance yourself from this sad situation, improve your service and your relationship with the business and make it much less likely that the organization will feel that a third party could do it better. As your management of IT services improves you will find yourself firmly in the Effective Supplier box and hopefully well on the way towards becoming a valued Business Partner, contributing directly to business performance and regarded as a strategic asset of the company. That is the vision; in the rest of this book we will outline how we think you can start to achieve it.

The Vision

Summary

- A small IT team has much to gain from the implementation of IT service management and is uniquely placed to achieve significant progress in a relatively short space of time – in fact, to timescales that will make their large company equivalents 'green with envy'.
- Key to this goal is the ability to interpret literature that is often aimed at larger organizations and to make it seem relevant and useful to a small team. This book has been written to help you towards this goal.
- The vision is to move from a Necessary Expense, through an Effective Supplier to become a true Business Partner.

2 The IT service management landscape

Overview

Before launching into an explanation of the various concepts surrounding IT service management, it is probably worth just quickly setting straight some of the terms about the subject. People often ask 'What is the difference between 'IT service management', 'ITIL', 'ISO/IEC 20000' and all the other terms bandied around in the industry?' So, here is a quick explanation.

IT service management is a discipline. It is a subject area supported by a significant amount of knowledge that is set out in books and other media and in people's heads. There are an infinite number of ways to do IT service management: the ITIL and the like are only documented examples of how it can be done – even if you are not aware of any of the methods below, if you are delivering IT services then you are doing IT service management already. The aim of ITIL, ISO/IEC 20000, COBIT, etc. is to help you to do it more effectively and with lower risk and, hopefully, lower cost.

ITIL (IT Infrastructure Library) is a series of books written and maintained by the OGC (UK Office of Government Commerce) that documents the collective view and experiences of many organizations' 'good practice' ways of performing IT service management activities. So you will find chapters on incident management, on release management, on capacity management, etc. This provides much of the detail about how to carry out IT service management activities, including process diagrams and roles and responsibilities, all brought together into an overall life cycle model. ITIL is often referred to as a 'framework' because it gives you the structure but it is up to you to tailor it at a lower level to your organization's specific requirements.

ISO/IEC 20000 is an international standard like ISO 9001 (quality management) or ISO 14001 (environmental management). It takes those aspects of IT service management that are deemed, by several international committees, as mandatory for an organization wishing to prove that they demonstrate good practice. All requirements of the standard (Part 1) should be complied with for the organization to be certified to ISO/IEC 20000. There are several other parts of ISO/IEC 20000

Overview

that deserve a mention: Part 2, the Code of Practice, elaborates on the necessarily minimalist requirements of Part 1 and describes to some extent how the processes should be implemented – useful if you would like more detail than is contained in Part 1 but don't want to read all five ITIL V3 books. Parts 3, 4 and 5 provide further guidance on scope definition, reference model and implementation respectively. There are also plans for a Part 8 (Process Assessment Model) and Part 10 (Concepts and Terminology), so ISO/IEC 20000 is fast developing into a well-rounded definition of IT service management good practice.

Figure 2 summarizes the structure and the general concepts of the ISO/IEC 20000 standard.

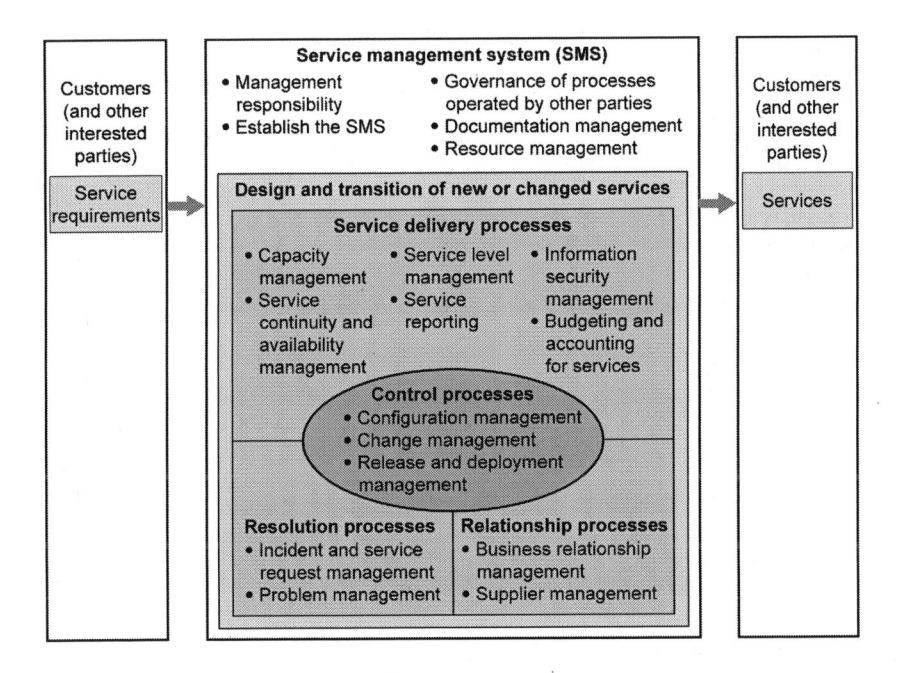

```
┌──────────────┐  ┌─────────────────────────────────────────────┐  ┌──────────────┐
│              │  │        Service management system (SMS)      │  │              │
│  Customers   │  │  • Management          • Governance of      │  │  Customers   │
│  (and other  │  │    responsibility        processes operated │  │  (and other  │
│  interested  │  │  • Establish the SMS     by other parties   │  │  interested  │
│  parties)    │  │                        • Documentation mgmt │  │  parties)    │
│              │  │                        • Resource management│  │              │
│              │  ├─────────────────────────────────────────────┤  │              │
│   Service    │→ │ Design and transition of new or changed     │→ │   Services   │
│ requirements │  │ services                                    │  │              │
│              │  │  ┌───────────────────────────────────────┐  │  │              │
│              │  │  │        Service delivery processes     │  │  │              │
│              │  │  │  • Capacity      • Service level      │  │  │              │
│              │  │  │    management      management         │  │  │              │
│              │  │  │  • Service       • Service reporting  │  │  │              │
│              │  │  │    continuity    • Information        │  │  │              │
│              │  │  │    and             security mgmt      │  │  │              │
│              │  │  │    availability  • Budgeting and      │  │  │              │
│              │  │  │    management      accounting for     │  │  │              │
│              │  │  │                    services           │  │  │              │
│              │  │  │         Control processes             │  │  │              │
│              │  │  │  • Configuration management           │  │  │              │
│              │  │  │  • Change management                  │  │  │              │
│              │  │  │  • Release and deployment management  │  │  │              │
│              │  │  ├─────────────────┬─────────────────────┤  │  │              │
│              │  │  │ Resolution      │ Relationship        │  │  │              │
│              │  │  │ processes       │ processes           │  │  │              │
│              │  │  │ • Incident and  │ • Business          │  │  │              │
│              │  │  │   service req   │   relationship mgmt │  │  │              │
│              │  │  │   management    │ • Supplier          │  │  │              │
│              │  │  │ • Problem mgmt  │   management        │  │  │              │
└──────────────┘  └─────────────────────────────────────────────┘  └──────────────┘
```

Figure 2 – Summary of the ISO/IEC 20000 standard

Source: ISO/IEC 20000:2011 Part 1

Previously ITIL and ISO/IEC 20000 have not absolutely correlated as there were processes specified in ITIL which did not exist in ISO/IEC 20000 (event management, for example), but the principles set out in ISO/IEC 20000 could still be used to fill the gaps for those missing processes. The ISO/IEC 20000 standard is constantly being reviewed and is revised every five or so years to keep it in line with good practice thinking. A revised version of Part 1 (the Requirements) of the

2 The IT service management landscape

ISO/IEC 20000 standard was published in 2011; one of the objectives of this new version is to realign the standard with ITIL V3 more fully.

To summarize and draw an academic parallel, it could broadly be said that 'IT service management' is the subject, ITIL is the set of knowledge that forms the content and ISO/IEC 20000 is the exam that you can choose to take at the end to prove your organization's proficiency in the subject.

A bit of history

There are a few things about ITIL that deserve a quick mention. It began life in the 1980s as the IT Infrastructure Library, a collection of 34 books covering aspects of managing IT operations. Titles ranged from the familiar *Change Management*, to guidance on Local Area Network (LAN) wiring and *Setting up a Machine Room*. The intention was to improve IT service quality in central and local government, and nationalized utilities. This was Version 1.

ITIL V2 was developed mainly in the late 1990s. It had a narrower focus, on the more familiar set of seven books and the associated topics (although most of the attention was typically put on the first two of these, known as the Red and Blue Books):

- service delivery (covering availability management, capacity management, financial management for IT services, IT service continuity management and service level management) – this was the Red Book;
- service support (covering configuration management, change management, incident management, problem management, release management and the service desk function) – the Blue Book;
- software asset management;
- security management;
- application management;
- infrastructure management;
- the business perspective.

ITIL started to spread worldwide and leap across the divide between public and private sector, The Netherlands having an especially prominent and active role. By around 2000, it had become the de facto standard for IT service management. The project to create ITIL V3, originally labelled as the 'ITIL Refresh', was announced in 2005 and it was published in May 2007. This consolidated the V2 guidance into a set of five books, one for each stage of a life cycle, consisting of:

1. Service strategy.
2. Service design.
3. Service transition.

4. Service operation.
5. Continual service improvement.

However, V3 was not an immediate replacement for V2 and even now there are many organizations using the V2 books as their main guidance. There has been some criticism around the readability of some of the V3 books and this has resulted in a partial rewrite, which is scheduled to hit the shelves during 2011.

The ITIL V3 Life cycle is normally represented with Service Strategy at the core and design, Transition and Operation guided by it. Continual Service Improvement is then shown as being applied across all of the processes. In addition to the five core books there is a wide variety of complementary publications also published by the OGC (Office of Government Commerce, the owners of ITIL) and a number of web-based initiatives available.

Associated concepts, models and tools

It is also worth taking a brief look at certain associated concepts which will help you to better understand the entire IT service management landscape – ITIL and ISO/IEC 20000 are far from the full story on IT service management. We have given a flavour of each of these in the section below but please look at Appendix B for more detail and references to some sources of information about each of them. Don't forget that these are simply other guidance models to which you might want to refer if it helps you and your organization reach your goals. Don't get too concerned with trying to use everything; cherry-pick those ideas and concepts that help you and ignore those that don't.

The **Capability Maturity Model Integration (CMMI)** is a model for assessing the processes of an organization against a stepped scale of 'maturity'. Used correctly the CMMI can be very useful in a gap assessment of an organization's IT service management processes (or indeed any of its processes).

ISO/IEC 27000 is a family of international standards that provide a good practice solution to a range of regulatory and operational security issues faced by organizations. It provides guidance on areas such as security policy, organization, personnel security, communications and operations management, access control, system development and maintenance, business continuity management, physical and environmental security and compliance.

COBIT stands for 'Control Objectives for Information and Related Technology', and is a model designed to address the control of the entire IT function. It was originally developed in 1994 by the research institute of the Information Systems Audit and Control Association (ISACA). It supports and assists management in the governance of IT by providing a comprehensive description of a series of control objectives for all IT processes and by providing a mechanism for monitoring, measuring and assessing the ongoing maturity of the processes.

ISO/IEC 38500 is an international standard describing a framework for the governance of the use of IT by an organization. This is subtly different from (but closely linked to) COBIT in that COBIT is a model for the governance of processes within IT whereas ISO/IEC 38500 is a model for how senior management (the board of directors or similar) should govern and set strategic direction for IT across the organization.

Lean is a continual improvement method, often described as a 'mindset', the core idea of which is to maximize customer value while minimizing waste. Lean simply means creating more value for customers with fewer resources. Within IT Lean has been a relatively recent entrant to the discussion, although it has been around in other industries, particularly manufacturing, for some time.

Six Sigma was originally developed in the mid-1980s by Motorola, as a way to measure and reduce the amount of variation or inconsistency in a process. It provides a quantitative methodology for continual improvement and lowering costs by reducing the amount of variation in process outcomes to a level suitable for the given organization.

Others

There are also several other frameworks, models and international standards that support various parts of IT service management, such as:

- Microsoft Operations Framework (MOF) – similar in scope to ITIL V3;
- BS 25999 British Standard for business continuity management – tipped to become an international standard in the not too distant future;
- ISO/IEC 19770 – an international standard for software asset management;
- ISO 9001 – a well-known general quality standard that forms the basis for many other standards including ISO/IEC 20000 and ISO/IEC 27001;
- TickIT – a software development standard, also closely related to ISO 9001.

Decisions, decisions ...

Although this book focuses quite heavily on the processes associated with IT service management, it is worth pointing out at an early stage that the actual aim of all of this is to deliver to the business the support that it requires. That doesn't just mean fixing PCs when needed; it involves providing the business with the means to deliver its goods or services to its customers in the most effective way. IT can be a huge enabler of this but only if the mindset is right. There's an oft-cited adage that people do not want quarter-inch drill bits, they want quarter-inch holes. We would contend that they actually want a place to keep their books – which is reliant on having a shelf, which is reliant on brackets, which need quarter-inch holes for the screws to support the brackets. In reality, the customer's perception of the value delivered by IT will be measured by how easy it is to perform its tasks. Please keep this in mind even when we are deep into the detail of a particular process.

So which of these various options should a manager of a small IT team use to help further his/her IT service management ambitions? Inevitably this is a difficult question. All of the frameworks, standards and methods outlined above have been created over a period of time by very clever people and, used correctly, will all help to improve the way in which you deliver IT services to your organization. One answer would be that you should try to take the best from each of the above options, but for a busy IT manager we recognize that this would be a very time-consuming approach and probably lead to a great deal of confusion for you and your staff.

So our recommendation is that you choose a single standard or framework as your main source of knowledge and run with it, using other sources if you wish as backup information to fill in the occasional gap or expand upon specific areas. This is the approach we have taken in writing this book and so we have had to come down on the side of one or two of the above methods in order to keep the subject logical and consistent.

For the record, then, the advice given within these pages is largely based upon the ISO/IEC 20000 standard, with further expansion supplied from the ITIL V3 framework. We could have used COBIT or MOF (or even ITIL V2) and so can you if you choose to. But, as we have already admitted, our combined experience leans towards ISO/IEC 20000 and ITIL V3 so we feel we can do a better job of explaining the ideas with these as a guide.

That said, let's start making some progress.

2   The IT service management landscape

Summary

- IT service management is a discipline for which ITIL is a body of knowledge detailing the collective view of good practice and ISO/IEC 20000 is a standard against which organizations can be certified.
- There are many associated concepts and models that can be useful in the IT Manager's arsenal including: CMMI for assessing maturity, ISO/IEC 27000 for assessing, controlling and certifying security, COBIT and ISO/IEC 38500 for asserting a manageable framework for both the governance of IT and of the processes of IT, Lean and Six Sigma for improvement and efficiency.
- The contents of this book are largely based upon the ISO/IEC 20000 standard and ITIL V3, but these are by no means the only options for improving your IT service management
- Our recommendation is that you choose a single standard or framework as your main source of knowledge and run with it, using other sources if you wish as backup.

Next step

Find out more about the frameworks, standards and methods covered to get a better idea of how they may be useful to you – see Appendix B for more information.

3 Planning for IT service management

The gap analysis

The great thing about good practice is that it defines pretty clearly where you need to end up. But to get from where you are now to the IT service management promised land you will need to know the first bit – where are you now? This is the purpose of the gap analysis (it may go by other names such as 'ITSM assessment' or 'maturity analysis' but it is basically the same thing). This is important because it gives you a clear idea of what will need to be done, how long it may take, the likely cost and, most important of all, what benefits you may derive from starting to do things differently.

Approach

There are really only two main ways of carrying out an IT service management gap analysis. First, you could get a consultant to do it for you. There are consultancy firms large and small who have carried out similar exercises many times before and would, of course, bring significant experience and advice to the party. But this comes at a price and it's up to you whether you think it's worth it and whether you have a budget available. Bear in mind that an external assessment is likely to carry more weight than one you have done yourself and will tend to be more objective, so it may well be worth the extra expenditure at the start.

Second, you could do it yourself. There are a number of gap analysis toolkits available that can assist you in this and it is worth having a look around on the internet to see if they meet your needs. Or you could make your own – and we will tell you how.

But what exactly will you be assessing the gap against? Again, there are options. Generally accepted good practice in IT service management is embodied in ITIL. In its latest version, ITIL V3 consists of five books covering each of the steps in a life cycle approach – namely Strategy, Design, Transition, Operation and Continual Service Improvement. So you could, in theory, look through the books in turn and try to assess to what extent you currently follow the processes they describe. This is certainly

3   Planning for IT service management

possible and may well be a worthwhile exercise if only because you will become familiar with the content of the books. But it may take you quite a while to do and the results will probably be a little subjective. So we'd like to propose an alternative way of doing it that in our view, is quicker, cheaper and more measurable than this approach.

Even if you have absolutely no intention of having your organization certified against it, comparing yourself against the international standard for IT service management, ISO/IEC 20000, is in our opinion easier than comparing yourself against ITIL because the former is much more concise, consisting of fewer than 20 pages of requirements versus many hundreds in ITIL. This means that it is perfectly feasible to go through ISO/IEC 20000 Part 1 (the Specification) line by line and decide whether or not each of the 200 or so requirements is currently in place. It is as though the ISO/IEC committee has done the hard work for you in distilling ITIL down into a short (but admittedly rather dry) concise summary of the best aspects of good practice.

There are published materials to help you take this approach (and we recommend you look at them) but you also have the option to save yourself some money and just import Part 1 (the Requirements) of the standard into a spreadsheet and work from that (of course, you will need to buy the standard first so it's not a completely cost-free option). Make sure that each requirement is listed in a separate cell so that you can indicate individually, using a 1 (Yes) or a 0 (No) whether it is followed within your organization. For those that you are not sure about we suggest you err on the side of caution and put a 0. This then allows you to objectively measure how much of good practice you are currently doing and to break it down by process area.

Add a few meaningful charts created from the spreadsheet data and you're in business! We've put an example in Appendix A.1 to give you an idea of what this could look like. It is also a good idea to record any supporting information or evidence for a 'Yes' and an action for each 'No'.

Doing it this way also means you can repeat the process on a regular basis throughout the project to keep track of how compliant with ISO/IEC 20000 you are to date. This also provides a great indicator to put in your weekly progress reports.

Method

The gap analysis is very similar to an audit in many ways and the methods used to carry it out are the same, namely:

- a review of documentation and records;

The gap analysis

- interviewing key personnel;
- observing the team in action.

The main difference between the gap analysis and a real audit is that the gap analysis is a complete 'drains up' exercise covering all areas of IT service management in which we want staff to volunteer information about how things are really done at the moment. We want all the issues to be laid bare so that we can obtain a true picture of how much work there is to do. An audit, in contrast, tends to be a slightly more guarded affair where staff largely stick to answering just the questions they are asked, and no more.

Although the three methods are listed below in a set order, in practice they need all to happen at the same time and build upon each other – for example, you interview a member of staff, review the records to confirm what he or she is saying, sit in and observe it happening then discuss your findings in another interview, followed by more observation, etc. This will then allow you to reach a considered conclusion for each requirement, along with supporting observations. If you are the IT Manager then, since your team is small, you may already be aware of most of the answers without consulting anyone else; but be careful to check that the way you think things happen is actually the way they happen on the ground.

Review of documentation and records

The first step is to gather together all the documentation you currently have into one place and assess it against what is required by the standard. You may have some that, although it doesn't have the same name as that in the standard, fulfils the same purpose so still counts. The documentation in existence often tends to be of a technical nature and is focused on a specific piece of technology. This may represent a record of some kind in ISO/IEC 20000 terms – for example, a procedure for allowing suppliers to access your servers remotely is not explicitly defined in the standard but is still relevant to the Information Security section as a 'control' that implements part of your information security policy (once you have one).

Many of your records may exist in your current service desk system in various guises and you may also have some form of knowledge base on a shared network drive. Documents produced as part of wider company processes, such as HR and budgeting, will also be relevant.

The key points to look for within your documentation set are:

- How complete is it? Are there any processes that are not documented?

3 Planning for IT service management

- Is it being used? Do all relevant staff know about the documentation and is there evidence that they are following it?
- Is it being kept up to date?
- Is it subject to change management?
- Does it contain control information such as version history, author, owner, distribution and approval?

Interviewing key personnel

For each part of the standard you need to identify who is currently responsible for that area. This may not be possible if some of the processes just don't exist at the moment, but if that is the case then try to pin down the person who is closest to it.

You then need to sit them down away from any distractions and have a chat. Emphasize that this is not an audit and that you actually want them to tell you what isn't right rather than a fantasy view of how they wish things were. Start by asking them to describe how things currently work in the area under discussion before moving on to discussing the requirements of the standard line by line. It may help to have your gap analysis spreadsheet open on a laptop and mark each requirement as you go along.

Ask them to show you the evidence of what they say is happening – for example, help desk records, reports, minutes of meetings, emails. If they cannot evidence it, the chances are it isn't really happening or it's so informal that it doesn't count. Of course, in a small team you, as the IT Manager or similar position, will probably wear many of the process owner hats and so be the person who needs to be interviewed. If you are using an external consultant then this will not be a problem as he or she can ask you the required questions. If you are doing the exercise yourself, however, then you just need to ensure that you are as honest and accurate as you can reasonably be; remember that this is not a test but a way of working out what needs to be done to improve your life and the support of the business.

Don't forget to talk to people other than the IT staff – there is no better place to get a true impression of user perception than from a real-life user or two.

Observing the team in action

This mainly applies to the Resolution processes (incident and problem management), but could also be carried out for other processes such as Relationship (by sitting in on some business and supplier meetings) and Control (sitting in on a Change Advisory Board meeting).

The gap analysis

The main place to start is the help/service desk, and then move into one or more of the second-line resolution groups (if you have them) such as desktop support. You are looking to see if the procedures are actually known about and followed (or kept in a locked filing cabinet in the basement), and whether some of the linkages between processes happen as the standard requires them to – e.g. between incident and problem management. You can pick up a lot of useful information just from loitering. Again, the fact that it's not a test needs to be emphasized to the staff being observed so that they continue to do things the way they normally do rather than the way they think you want them to.

Remember to take timed and dated notes of what has been observed for reference later.

Analysing and presenting the results

Once you have reviewed your documentation, interviewed the key staff members, observed the delivery of the service in action and recorded your results on your assessment spreadsheet, it is time to create the gap analysis report. This is a key document that, if prepared properly, will fulfil a number of purposes:

- a snapshot that tells you how compliant your organization currently is to good practice;
- supporting evidence for your proposal to senior management to implement good practice;
- a roadmap for you and your team for the project to go forward.

As a minimum, the gap analysis report needs to answer the following key questions:

- What benefits could we and the organization obtain by doing things in accordance with good practice?
- How close to the ISO/IEC 20000 standard are we at the moment?
- What approach should we take to implement IT service management?
- How long is it likely to take?
- How much will it cost?
- Where should we start?
- Do we need to buy a new tool(s)?
- How much effort do we as an IT team need to put in?
- What will we need from the business to make it work?

The trick in the report is to keep the answers as simple as possible. If, as we suggested, you have used a spreadsheet to assess yourself against the requirements, then you will be able to give a straight percentage figure for how close you are, backed up by a chart that shows a percentage broken down by area of the standard (see Figure 3). It will not be

3 Planning for IT service management

infallible but it will give everyone a pretty good idea of where you stand, which is all that is required at this stage.

Small IT Team Ltd.
% Complying with ISO 20000

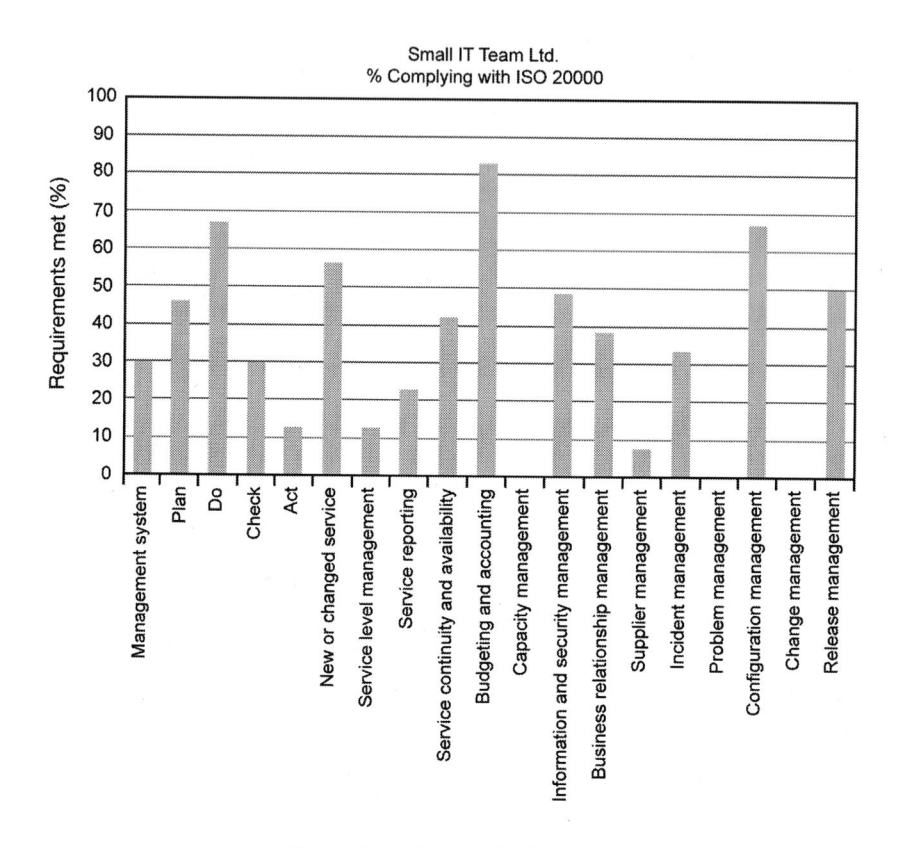

[Bar chart showing Requirements met (%) for: Management system, Plan, Do, Check, Act, New or changed service, Service level management, Service reporting, Service continuity and availability, Budgeting and accounting, Capacity management, Information and security management, Business relationship management, Supplier management, Incident management, Problem management, Configuration management, Change management, Release management]

Figure 3 – Gap analysis chart

Within the report don't forget to include those things that you are currently doing right as well as areas for improvement so that a balanced view is presented to the reader, who may well be your manager or director. Some input from the business will also help to ensure the report is a balanced view of where you are now. In terms of timescales it may be useful to talk to other IT managers who have implemented good practice within an organization of your size, and remember to factor in the upcoming projects that you are aware of which may act as a drain on resources and divert you from your goal.

Summary

- We recommend comparing your current IT service management processes against Part 1 of the ISO/IEC 20000 standard (the Requirements).
- The gap analysis is carried out via a combination of interview, document review and observation.
- The resulting report needs to answer all of the key questions such as why, when, how, who and how much?

Next steps

1. Decide whether you will do the gap analysis yourself or get someone in to do it.
2. Carry out the gap analysis.
3. Report and present the results

Gaining management commitment

So, let's say that you're convinced: IT service management good practice is the way forward for organizing the activities your small IT team performs to achieve efficient and effective service delivery. You are convinced, but now for the tough crowd – the senior management.

You will need to provide a costed forecast of how this new set-up will be implemented, how long it's going to take (both in terms of elapsed time and man-hours) and what the risks are (both of doing it and of not doing it). But the most important factor is what you intend it to achieve: things like cost savings, improved quality and reliability, faster delivery (of new services, of changes) and better ability to adapt to the changing business needs.

This all sounds rather daunting and, in some parts, nigh on impossible but, fear not, it's really a simple process of assembling facts. To begin with, you really need to understand the problem. The first step is to perform a gap assessment on your operation and we have explained how to do this in the previous section.

3   Planning for IT service management

Baselining current service

Next, you need to baseline a series of key metrics. Basically this means putting a stake in the ground to define – and, most importantly, quantify – where you are starting from. This is essential as it is against these metrics you will promise improvement and, further down the line, report your progress to management. A typical set may be as follows.

- User satisfaction – run a survey if you don't already; check that any existing survey asks questions that are relevant to the delivery of current IT services.
- Staff satisfaction and morale – use the most recent employee survey if there is one; if not you could create your own.
- Service levels – is there a commonly understood informal Service Level Agreement (SLA) that determines existing user expectations? What levels of service are currently being delivered (e.g. average incident resolution times, average phone answer times on the help desk)?
- Staffing levels – mix of permanent and contract staff; staff turnover rates; number of incidents resolved per staff member per day/week.
- Number of incidents being reported and closed – you will need some historical data to allow for seasonal fluctuations (e.g. quiet holiday period).
- Number of failed changes – this may be hard to identify, but try to look back at any major incidents you have had over the last three to six months and determine whether they happened because something was changed.
- Service availability – particularly for your most critical systems, how many outages have you had in the last six to twelve months and how long did they last? How much did they cost the company in lost production?
- And, of course, cost – how much do you currently spend on delivering live services? How is it broken down?

Once you have your gap assessment and metrics, you can begin the process of putting together two things:

1. A Service Management Plan – what are you trying to achieve and how are you going to do it?
2. A business case to convince senior management – why is it a good idea? Is any required investment justified?

So, let's tackle each of these in turn.

The IT Service Management Plan

This is simply a document detailing what aspects of IT service management you are planning to tackle, in what order and how. It doesn't need to be particularly fancy; it may be as simple as:

1. a section detailing the overall rationale and aims – for example, to reduce costs and improve customer and user satisfaction whilst maintaining the IT function as an in-house team;
2. a section explaining what the desired objectives are (with timescales), for example:
    (a) reduce overall IT spend by 5 per cent by end of Q4;
    (b) increase quantity of help desk incidents fixed at first call by 10 per cent within one year;
    (c) improve user satisfaction rating from X to Y by end of Q2Y2;
    (d) increase the availability of critical systems by 2 per cent;
    (e) reduce the number of incidents reported by 5 per cent.
3. a brief section explaining the approach being used:
    (a) six-monthly self-assessments against ISO/IEC 20000 to generate;
    (b) a score for each process that will be used to revise the strategy;
    (c) you should include here details of how the progress will be governed and monitored.
4. a list of all of the IT service management processes in ISO/IEC 20000 detailing:
    (a) the current and desired maturity levels; and
    (b) prioritization accorded to each process (some may factor more heavily towards your overall aims or objectives – see 'Planning considerations' in the next section).

For each process, detail what needs to be changed, improved or implemented about the process in order to achieve the desired maturity rating you have determined in your plan. You should also consider each of the metrics that you have set as your objectives and detail the actions that need to be taken in order to bring about the improvement.

Against each of the listed actions you need to be able to put a reasonable estimate of how long this is likely to take, who needs to be involved and how much of their time needs to be spent on it. You also need to include any tools or external goods or services that need to be bought or brought in to assist in the implementation (e.g. a configuration management database, any training courses for IT or user staff, external consultants for assistance or consultancy). These should all be priced and given timescales.

The overall plan is probably best shown as a series of spreadsheets, one per process, showing a Gantt chart of the actions to be taken, although by all means use a project management tool if you are confident in its use.

3 Planning for IT service management

Planning considerations

But which of the many and varied processes of IT service management should you spend time on first? The answer obviously depends to some extent on where you're starting from, but for the sake of simplicity we will assume that you currently have none of the processes in place. You may have one or more particular areas that are causing you the most pain – such as a high rate of failed changes or constantly running out of disk space – in which case you should certainly address those first as they will be where you will derive the most benefit (and you may choose to define these, using that slightly overused term, as the quick win). You may also have external drivers that dictate where to start, such as a negative audit report or instructions from senior management.

External influences apart, although many of the processes are closely related to each other, you do have the option to start wherever you need to, since few of them are so tightly coupled that they absolutely must be done together – change and configuration management is the most often quoted example of closely related processes and it would certainly be wise to approach these as a pair. Those aside, you may decide to address the processes one at a time or to some extent in parallel, depending on how much time you have available. Some organizations implement the processes according to the ITIL V3 groupings of Strategy, Design, Transition, Operation and Continual Service Improvement, although the order can vary widely depending on perceived priorities. This is also a valid approach but requires a bit more knowledge about how ITIL V3 is structured to make it work. The recommendation of ISO/IEC 20000 Part 5 'Exemplar Implementation Plan' is that the reactive processes are addressed first before moving on to the proactive ones and that would seem to make a lot of sense.

Our usual recommendation, based on experience, is that you begin with the most visible and easy to relate to process, namely incident management. This underpins many of the other processes and, because it usually involves a significant proportion of the IT team, there is a lot to be gained from improving its effectiveness early. It also usually exists already in some form so really you will be improving a process rather than shocking your staff with a completely new one. It is best to ease good practice into your team rather than hitting them over the head with it. Another advantage of starting here is that any improvement will be noticed straight away by your users, so providing extra momentum to keep going.

In good practice terms, the process of incident management is normally run by the function of the IT service desk and if you don't already have one of these this is a good time to start to think about establishing one. If the incident (and service request) volume justifies it you may decide to have one or more members of your team allocated to the service desk full-time, perhaps even on a rota basis. But if volume is low and your

Gaining management commitment

team is very small then you will need to juggle the response to incidents around other work, possibly by encouraging users to log incidents via a self-service method (or simply email) rather than by telephone.

Building on this foundation, the next area to address is usually problem management as this can have a significant effect on reducing the number of incidents logged by working out why they happen in the first place. It is also closely related to incident management so it appears to be a logical step to the rest of the IT team, so reducing resistance. Once these two processes are implemented you will be well on your way, and hopefully the benefits of using good practice will be starting to become clear.

Next on your list will typically be change, release and configuration management as these also relate closely to incident and problem management and are most likely to be implemented using the same service desk system. It is worth pointing out that the often-quoted triangle of 'People/Process/Technology' still applies to IT service management just as it does to most areas of IT (although ITIL V3 adds a fourth element of 'Partners'), and you need to ensure that each of these aspects is addressed in a balanced way – see the section headed 'The people aspects' and Chapter 8 relating to tools for some ideas on how to do that.

In ITIL V3 terms this means that you will by now have addressed most areas of Service Operation and Service Transition. In the past many organizations have effectively stopped when these processes are in place, regarding their project as complete. Experience has shown, however, that pressing on to the remaining processes brings significant benefits and you should aim to keep the momentum you have built up. With initial processes in place you will have established control over your environment and can begin to measure and report on service levels with a view to setting targets in a Service Level Agreement.

By this point in your project you should be more experienced in good practice and can pick and choose which areas to cover next; we would hesitate to suggest any particular order as it really does depend upon where your weak spots are, but a typical sequence might be:

1. Budgeting and accounting
2. Business relationship management
3. Supplier management
4. Availability/service continuity
5. Information security management
6. Capacity and performance management

As we said earlier, doing them all in parallel is also quite achievable, depending on how much time you have available. You should be finding

3 Planning for IT service management

that the information flowing from the processes you have already implemented smoothes the way for those coming afterwards.

The business case

So, you have thought through what ITSM needs to achieve; you now have details of the problem (nature and scale), the recommended solution and the costs of implementing the solution. What you now need is a way to convince senior management to let you do it – you need a business case.

ITIL defines this as 'justification for a significant item of expenditure, including information about costs, benefits, options, issues, risks and possible problems'. It is basically a vehicle for you to explain the aims of the initiative, how you're proposing to approach it, what the various pros and cons are of the proposed options and what commitment you are asking for from the senior management team (in terms of cost and support). In an ideal world, no project should be undertaken in business without a clear idea of the costs, risks and anticipated returns and benefits.

Senior management need to be made aware of what you are entering into, especially as IT service management is much more than implementing a new technology or relocating an office: it is about changing to a new way of working that will continue well after the initial 'flush' of the implementation is over, so you need senior management to be fully bought-in to it.

A typical business case will contain:

1. Introduction – this presents the business objectives that the project, initiative or investment is hoping to address.
2. Methods and assumptions – the main body of the business case, laying out the options considered and proposed and the assumptions that underpin and limit the scope of the business case.
3. Business impacts – an explanation of the financial and non-financial effects the business case may have on the business.
4. Risks and contingencies – the probability that alternative results will emerge and how it is anticipated to deal with them.
5. Recommendations – the option preferred, specific actions required and next steps.

The introduction

The introduction should be the easy bit (relatively). What are the issues facing your department? What are the resultant issues to the business, to the services you deliver, to your users and customers and, ultimately, to the customers of your organization?

When you're writing the business case, you might find that the scale of the problem is (or at least looks on paper) daunting. At this point you should step back a little and ask yourself 'what are the key issues that need to be tackled first?'. This will allow you to limit the initial scope of your implementation and break the whole exercise into more manageable phases (eating the elephant one bite at a time). This will also have the beneficial effect that you can show early returns on senior management faith in your plans.

Be brief, but make sure that all the points are there, are well explained and are relevant to your audience. Go through the points with a colleague from the business to make sure that he or she agrees with the points you are making; there is nothing worse than putting a report in front of the board and having it blown apart for want of better background research.

Methods and assumptions

This is where you can start to lay out your plan. Begin by explaining, briefly, what it is you are proposing. Don't fill the report with too much explanation – you can take along or supply backup information as you think fit, but don't include it all here. What you want is to paint a full picture of how your proposal is going to address all of the issues you identified in the introduction.

Make sure that you highlight clearly the costs, timescales and any other investments you require to make it work. For example, you may need the board to agree to include compliance with IT service management policies into everyone's personal performance objectives. If this is part of a longer, phased approach, explain that and give a sketch idea of how the rest of the plan will look.

In addition to your plan, you also need to detail at least one other option that could be considered. This may be the 'Do nothing' option, that indicates to the management the costs and risks associated with not following your recommended course of action. There may be other ways of achieving the same results but at a higher cost (outsourcing or getting a slew of consultants in to do the work). You should give sufficient detail to show that you have not overlooked them.

3 Planning for IT service management

You need to be clear, concise and honest. Failing on any of these counts will at best cause you problems and at worst get the business case dismissed.

Business impacts, risks and contingencies

These two sections are what will really matter to the senior management: how will your proposals affect, positively or negatively, the smooth operation of their business? Will it add to productivity? If so, how and by how much? Will it allow them to reduce head count? Will it reduce the cost of IT? Will it reduce the amount of time the sales team have to wait for quotations? WIIFM ... What's In It For Me?

Be as business-minded as possible and make sure you explain the impacts in terms that the senior management will clearly understand. Think about the whole plan from their perspective and think through 'what will happen if ...' and 'how will this affect ...' from the point of view of a department manager, a team leader, a call-centre operator and the end customers. If you show that you have really thought about how this can assist the business, rather than just expressing it as a series of benefits to the IT department, you will have gone a long way towards winning them over.

Recommendations

Obviously, you're going to recommend your preferred course of action, but you need to explain why. Why is this option the one that the management team should endorse? Make it clear and finish with a few statements explaining that option 1 (or 2, or 3) is your recommendation and what you want from the management team in order to get going.

An IT service management business case

So that's the process for putting a business case together, but what additional things should you be putting into a business case specifically for IT service management? The following is a non-exhaustive list put together from our experiences.

Direct costs

There are a number of costs that you can generally expect to incur with an IT service management implementation:

Gaining management commitment

- *ITSM software tools* – if you don't have a product already in use that can handle the additional things you want it to do then you will most likely be looking at an upgrade or replacement.
- *Hardware* – additional software may well need hardware on which to run.
- *Consultancy* – depending upon how much time you yourself have available to perform current state assessments and how confident you are to proceed without external advice.
- *Audit days* – if you intend to reach the ISO/IEC 20000 level, you will need to budget for the initial assessment days and for annual surveillance audits. Even if you're not, consider accounting for them to allow you to use an external pair of eyes on a yearly basis to perform your internal audits.
- *Training* – you may decide to allow a cost for each member of the IT team to be put through ITIL or ISO/IEC 20000 foundation training, or at least an overview course. You should also consider providing higher level (intermediate) courses for those individuals who will be assisting you with writing and maintaining the processes. In addition, you need to cost in your own intermediate or expert level training (or whoever will be driving the implementation forward).
- *Publications* – it would certainly be highly advantageous to have a full set of the ITIL manuals, and there will be many other publications which would be valuable additions to your IT service management library. If you decide to go for ISO/IEC 20000 certification you will also need to buy a copy of the standard, or at least Part 1 (Requirements) and ideally Part 2 (Code of Practice).

Time

Changing the way you and your organization work takes time, in terms of both man-days and elapsed days.

- Writing process documentation – do not underestimate how long it can take to write this as the first draft will, almost certainly, be too aspirational and several rewrites will generally be needed.
- QA of all documentation – every process document, every procedure and every policy that is written should be Quality Assured. A structured QA is the preferred method but this is not always possible so it should at least be read by an independent person to check for consistency, spelling, grammar, etc. Better still, that person should perform a 'sanity check' on the document to ensure that there are no glaring or fundamental flaws in the logic.
- Raising awareness – you will need to set aside a fair amount of time for each process-owner to get out there and raise awareness, both their own and that of the technical teams and users across the business.

3 Planning for IT service management

Risks

Consideration needs to be given to what could go wrong with the project and what to do if it does. Typical risks may be:

- lack of buy-in from staff;
- lack of senior management commitment;
- insufficient resources available to progress the project, perhaps as a result of unexpected business-critical projects;
- inadequate tools to support the processes;
- process introduction proves to be more complex than first thought.

Benefits

The expected benefits of improving IT service management need to be clear from the outset. This is often a difficult area to quantify as many of the benefits are qualitative, but it will help your project as well as your business case if specific targets are set (i.e. numbers). We have touched on this already in the setting of objectives in your IT Service Management Plan, but further examples could include the following.

- Cost reduction – fewer staff will be needed to provide the same level of service; use of contractors may be reduced.
- Reduction in the number of incidents logged and a corresponding increase in user productivity – you will need to do some research on business cost per incident to be able to quantify this.
- Increased availability of IT services – similarly you will need to calculate the cost per hour of an outage of a key service.
- Better alignment of IT services with business needs – less wasted effort in providing things users neither need nor want.
- Reduced risk to the business as a result of more effective security controls, capacity planning, etc.
- Improved value for money from existing suppliers and contracts.

Summary

- An IT service management plan sets out your objectives and approach and defines the activities, resources and timescales needed to meet your objectives.
- A business case is a useful tool for making the justification for IT service management improvement in your organization clear and achieving senior management buy-in.

- It should cover the introduction, methods and assumptions, business impacts, risks and contingencies, and recommendations concerned with your proposed IT service improvement project.
- Don't forget to budget for training, publications, consultancy (optional) and (if you decide to go for ISO/IEC 20000 certification) audit costs.
- You need to be clear, concise and honest. Failing on any of these counts will at best cause you problems and at worst get the business case dismissed.

Next steps

1. Start to think about what you are trying to achieve within your organization; how will it benefit the business, the IT team and other stakeholders?
2. Create a first draft IT service management plan in order to start to define your ideas of how it will work.
3. Draft a business case and obtain some feedback from suitable contacts or colleagues before submitting it to senior management.

The people aspects

As part of your good practice project you will be creating documents, perhaps installing some extra software and starting to measure quite a few things you didn't before. All of this is important, but make sure that the 'people aspects' of your implementation don't get overlooked. Be in no doubt, a service improvement project based around IT service management good practice is first and foremost a culture change project. If you don't have your team on side very little will change on the ground. Yes, you will have a more complete set of documentation and maybe even some great new software but, unless your people change the way they work day-to-day, the service to your users will stay exactly the same as before and you will have wasted a significant part of your time.

In this section we will look at how you can assess your skill and training requirements, measure and improve your team morale, involve your staff and possibly reorganize them into a more logical structure. But before we do this we'd like to say a few words about fostering genuine ownership of the new ways of working.

3 Planning for IT service management

All too often the way in which IT service management processes are introduced is by calling a meeting, showing a few slides of a process flowchart (probably copied from an ITIL book or similar) and then declaring this to be 'the new way we do things here'. Understandably this can cause a negative reaction (or worse, complete apathy) from the IT staff involved and the process is largely doomed before it has begun.

We would suggest that a better approach is to start with a discussion about the issues with the current process (perhaps using the brainstorming technique) and then work through how these issues may be addressed by creating a better process, mapping that process out as you go along. The last step would then be to compare that process with documented good practice (for example, in ITIL) to see if there are any areas that differ. But even if there are differences, don't assume that good practice will win through every time; the whole idea of frameworks such as ITIL is that they should be adapted to suit your particular organization. This is how the generic definition of 'good practice' in the books evolves into a specific implementation of 'best practice' within your team.

The point about introducing change in this way is that it answers the big question of 'why?', which is so often the stumbling block to the introduction of a better way of working. It also ensures that the people who create the new process are the very people best placed to get it right, namely those currently doing it. The ITIL books point out that the whole idea is to create 'practical solutions' not 'perfect processes'.

But what if you need to introduce a process that doesn't currently exist within your team? How can people come up with improvements if there is no starting point? The answer is that the vast majority of IT service management processes do in fact exist; they are just (sometimes very) informal. Take change management, for example: all IT teams change things – it's inevitable. So there is an existing process, but it may simply consist of the following steps:

1. Identify something that needs to be changed.
2. Change it.
3. Hope there are no undesirable consequences.

If you start from this process flow, and then work through with your team what else they perhaps should be doing, you may be surprised how quickly the main elements of good practice are suggested; but the ownership of the new process lies with your staff, not the authors of ITIL, COBIT or ISO/IEC 20000. We humbly suggest you use the books as guidelines, not dogma.

Within the field of business change management (as opposed to IT change management, which we discuss in Chapter 5 there are a number of well-known approaches to facilitating and embedding change that

The people aspects

you could look to use within your team. We only mention them briefly here but it is well worth finding out more about them.

The ADKAR model defines five factors to be created or developed when making changes:

- Awareness – about why the change is necessary;
- Desire – to co-operate and participate;
- Knowledge – to guide the change process;
- Ability – and relevant skills to drive the change process;
- Reinforcement – and plans to sustain the change process.

ITIL V3 recommends the use of John P. Kotter's *Eight Steps to Transforming Your Organisation* as follows:

1. Creating a sense of urgency.
2. Forming a guiding coalition.
3. Creating a vision.
4. Communicating the vision.
5. Empowering others to act on the vision.
6. Planning for and creating short-term wins.
7. Consolidating improvements and producing more change.
8. Institutionalizing the change.

But however you decide to approach the issue of change within your team it is important that you demonstrate some clear leadership, negotiation and listening skills to ensure that your people come with you on the journey rather than getting off at the first stop.

Skills and training

We have already stated that in a small IT team your people are your main asset. The reliance on the individual that being small entails makes having the right mix of skills to support your services an important issue. How do you build and maintain a clear picture of whether you've got it right?

Once you have a good idea of the services that you provide to your customers and have established a service catalogue, we would recommend that you give some thought as to the skills you need to have in your team to provide those services and conduct a training needs analysis, or TNA. For example, for an email service you may need your team to have skills in some or all of the following:

- the email client on the PC;
- the server email software;
- Domain Name Services (DNS);
- the operating system it runs on;

3 Planning for IT service management

- the hardware that provides the platform.

But have they? And, if so, how many of them have these skills and in what mixes? To find out you could review past training records or ask them to take some form of test, but that would be difficult and time-consuming. We would contend that the most effective way of finding out is simply to ask them.

First, you will need a list of skills such as those in the example above. Again, the most effective way to create such a list is to involve your team. Hold a workshop (see the section 'Methods of involvement' and get your team to tell you:

- all of the skills they can think of that they currently have;
- those skills that they don't have but believe are needed to support the services in the service catalogue (give everyone a copy of this to help things along).

Don't forget to cover both technical (e.g. operating systems, databases and hardware) and soft skills such as customer service, ITIL and training. Add any others you can think of yourself and then record and categorize the list however you see fit.

Now we need to understand how many people in your team have these skills and to what level. This is best done by creating a simple questionnaire (a spreadsheet will do) and using a basic rating system (e.g. 1 for no knowledge through to 5 for guru). Get each of your staff members (and yourself) then to rate themselves on each skill according to your rating scheme. Collect the responses (make sure everyone does it), perform a sanity check based on your own knowledge of your staff and do a simple spreadsheet analysis to assess the skill level within your team, both:

- as an average – this indicates the general level of knowledge in that area; and
- in terms of how many people you have above the level you feel is needed for that skill.

This second point is important as it will show you where you have single points of failure in the skills of your team; these often show up when a senior manager wants something done when the person who normally does it is on holiday and no one else in your team has a clue. The level you feel is needed will be dictated by how critical the services that rely on that skill are. For example, for your main business-critical system you will probably want at least two people with a skill level of 3 or more – just make sure they don't go on holiday at the same time.

Out of this analysis then falls your training requirements, based on the needs of your services and customers rather than what's cool to learn

The people aspects

about this year. You will probably have a mixture of training needs, some of which can be addressed by basic shadowing or team demonstrations rather than formal training. Repeat the exercise whenever you feel it's appropriate, maybe annually.

Lastly, it's worth mentioning SFIA. The Skills Framework for the Information Age is a simple and logical two-dimensional framework consisting of, on one axis, the skills in categories and subcategories and, on the other, the various levels of skill that can be attained. It is maintained by the SFIA Foundation, a not-for-profit organization to which the British Computer Society and the IT Service Management Forum subscribe. SFIA provides a common reference model for the identification of the skills needed to develop effective information systems (IS) making use of information communications technologies (ICT).

The purpose of SFIA is to provide a standardized view of the wide range of professional skills needed by people working in information technology. The definitions describe elements of required capability such as 'database design', rather than technologically-orientated matters such as the knowledge of a particular database. It uses a common language and a sensible, logical structure that can be adapted to the training and development needs of a very wide range of businesses – or simply used 'off the shelf'. It is worth a look to see if it might be useful for your team.

Improving morale

Is your IT team a bit fed up? One of the most common attributes of an IT department that hasn't implemented IT service management good practice is low morale. This can exhibit itself in many different ways, including regular complaints, open criticism of management and higher than average absence rates. There may also be a strong sense of distrust and cynicism, so when you start talking about IT service management you may not get a warm feeling that you're being listened to. Initially the only thing you can do is grit your teeth and work through it, but over time there are a number of actions you can take that will help to improve morale amongst your team. What they mostly come down to is showing that you actually care about your staff.

Some of the actions you can take are:

- *Praise* – catch them doing something right and make a fuss about it. Get your manager to come down and make a fuss about it too. Maybe even give them a certificate that says 'Well done'. It has to be genuine and deserved though: a certificate for 'making a great cup of tea' will undermine your credibility somewhat. Also, try to ensure that the behaviour you reward moves your team closer to achieving

3 Planning for IT service management

your objectives – if it can be related to Key Performance Indicators (KPIs) then everyone should be content.
- *Do performance reviews when you're supposed to* – nothing says 'I don't care about you' quite so well as not having a performance review for several years when they should be every six months. It's amazing how worthwhile everyone says they are if you actually make the effort.
- *Give them some training* – this also shows that your team is worth investing in as well as reducing the potential excuses for not doing something 'because I haven't been trained in it'. But don't promise what you can't deliver – if you haven't got the budget then be honest and look at lower-cost alternatives to classroom courses.
- *Communicate, communicate, communicate* – make sure you have weekly team meetings to tell your staff what's going on and to give them a chance to tell you what they think. Do your best to actually listen to what they're saying too, and then act on it. Always record the actions and come back to them next week. Be prepared for the first few meetings to be moaning sessions – it will improve over time, so stick with it

As with many aspects of service improvement, if you can't measure it, you can't improve it and team morale is no different. Many organizations now undertake employee satisfaction surveys and compare the results year upon year. If yours does this, then it can a very useful source of information not only about how satisfied your IT staff are, but whether the improvements you put in place have had any noticeable effect upon their satisfaction levels. If no survey exists at the moment then it is in your power to carry one out, focused specifically on the IT team. We would suggest that you undertake this prior to any improvement activities (to baseline team satisfaction) and then afterwards to see what improvement, if any, has been experienced. This could simply take the form of five to ten direct questions regarding areas such as overall happiness levels, communication, team spirit, career prospects and ability to do the job, perhaps rated on a simple 1–10 scale. Make room for free-text comments too as these are often more enlightening than the numbers. It doesn't need to be complicated, and in many ways just the act of carrying out a survey can have a positive effect on morale.

Methods of involvement

We've all had the experience – you hold a meeting to get people's views on a subject but most of them sit there looking at the floor, too fed up or too shy to contribute and all you get is one or two opinions from the same old people. So how do you actually get your staff involved in such meetings, workshops, etc.? The answer is sticky notes such as Post-its®

The people aspects

Now, we appreciate that these get a bad press nowadays largely from overuse. But if you need to make people contribute then they are your silver bullet (bear with us).

Brainstorming

(Also known by various other names such as 'mind sweeping' and 'thought shower'). An old technique and often misconstrued as an uncontrolled shouting out of ideas, but used correctly (and combined with sticky notes this simple method will make your staff feel that they have contributed and been listened to. We have used this successfully on many occasions where we need to pull ideas out of people.

Sit everyone in an arc around you and explain the subject of the brainstorm – you need to be fairly specific in order to get useful ideas. Write it down on a flipchart if you can. Example subjects might be 'What can we do to improve our incident management?' or 'How can we increase user satisfaction?'

State the rules, which are:

1. Keep strictly to the order – no one is allowed to shout out unless it's their turn.
2. Everyone gets a go.
3. You can pass if you have to, but try not to.

Then start at the first person and go round-robin fashion, writing each idea down on a sticky note as you go along. If some people keep passing, give them some gentle encouragement to contribute more. It works best with around ten people, give or take three or so: too many and people lose focus, too few and no one has enough time to think. When you get to the stage where most people are passing, open it up to everyone for any remaining ideas.

Clustering

This technique follows on from brainstorming. Once you have all the ideas written on sticky notes work with the group to cluster them together into common groups – for example, if the question was 'How can we improve IT staff skill levels?' then 'more courses' and 'better project handovers' could be grouped together. Once you have done this, ask the group to give each grouping a name (e.g. 'training').

You then have a set of ideas grouped into subject areas. The next step is to ask who will take ownership of each labelled grouping and, once this is decided, write that person's name next to the grouping.

3   Planning for IT service management

Follow-up

A key point about this area, in common with many others we will cover, is that you must document it. Record all of the sticky notes in their groupings with names and owners in an electronic document and then send it out to everyone who attended. Add the actions into your service improvement plan (we make no apologies for saying this time and time again as it is absolutely key).

The above techniques will provide an element of structure to your discussions and ensure that it's not just the loud ones who have a say in how your team develops. We're not suggesting you use this in every session but every now and then it is fine.

Organization structure

One of the questions often asked when implementing IT service management good practice is 'Should we change our IT organization structure?' It's an interesting point as existing working practices are often aligned and constrained by the structure of the team and role descriptions may be too specific (or in some cases we have come across, too generic) to allow much flexibility. In many ways it is best to delay making any significant changes until your good practice implementation is well underway; you may find that the IT staff themselves start to suggest role changes as the project progresses.

In the longer term the answer is ideally 'Yes' so that it fits the ITIL model (although now the debate is 'which ITIL model, V2 or V3?') but in reality it can be an area full of pitfalls for the unwary IT manager and often takes a long time to come to fruition. As soon as you suggest changing any titles or reporting lines a whole plethora of issues bubble to the surface, such as:

- Will we just slot into the new roles or will we have to apply for them?
- Do the unions need to be involved?
- What pay scales will the new roles have?
- Will they be advertised externally?
- What qualifications will I need to have for the new role?
- Will my sickness record count against me if I apply for a role?

It is clear from the above list of questions that you will need to get your human resources department (if you have one) involved from the outset to ensure you stay on the right side of employment law.

So, unless you're a very small company and you happen to be the owner, don't expect any quick fixes here. It's also not an absolute requirement of good practice – as long as your roles and responsibilities are defined and

The people aspects

allocated to someone—you'll be OK. The benefits of remoulding the organization structure are that you can be more specific with the IT service management roles and allocate them to people who have titles that reflect the area(s) they are concentrating on. This increases the likelihood of the processes being kept up to date once the excitement of the initial implementation has faded.

Of course, the amount of flexibility you have depends upon the size of your team – if it is very small then there is no alternative but to wear many hats at once (e.g. Incident Manager, Problem Manager, Change Manager) and make the best of it. This actually isn't as bad as it sounds because what you lose through lack of resource you will make up in lack of conflict between the roles (unless you like arguing with yourself).

If you do decide to change your organization structure then you have a number of options. The traditional way of organizing a small department around ITIL principles is to go with a straight service support/service delivery split in line with ITIL V2. This effectively means that one part of your team takes on the customer/user-facing aspects of the service including incident, problem and service level management, whilst the other concentrates more on the back-office processes such as capacity planning, information security and service continuity. In a small team this is often a sensible split and can make the most of an individual's specific talents (although beware of organizing your structure around personalities rather than service requirements).

With the advent of ITIL V3 the debate has increased in complexity. In theory a reasonable split would seem to be around the five areas of the life cycle – Strategy, Design, Transition, Operation and Continual Service Improvement (CSI) – but we have yet to see that work well in a small team environment (but in time it may). ITIL gives various suggestions but obviously cannot make firm recommendations as organizations are so diverse. Assuming that Strategy and CSI fall to the IT Manager, the three main areas most small IT teams struggle to organize around are projects, support and applications, particularly the first two. Applications support tends to be separated logically by its nature and few small IT teams nowadays do any significant bespoke applications development, so the main discussion is usually around how to cater for projects and ongoing support. Having been through a few nightmares of trying to allow support staff to participate in projects, our recommendation would be that they are considered separate roles to be performed by different people. Rotas of one day/week/month on projects followed by time on support sound good in that they make support staff aware of projects and enhance their skills, but rarely work effectively in practice. Keeping them separate also provides a defined career path to support staff.

3 Planning for IT service management

So by all means look at changing the structure of your IT team to fit the roles of IT service management but consider the issues carefully and if you are trying to implement processes quickly then don't expect it to happen at the same pace.

Summary

- Base your training programme on the skills needed to support your services via a skills audit.
- There are various techniques that can be used to improve morale within your IT team, including regular praise, ensuring reviews happen, taking training seriously and spending time on proper communication.
- Baselining your IT team's morale level at the start of a service improvement project may be useful so that the effect of improvements on morale can be objectively measured
- Brainstorming and clustering using sticky notes can be an effective technique for involving all of your staff.
- Restructuring your IT team around IT service management principles may be useful but give it plenty of thought first, involve HR and don't expect it to happen quickly.

Next steps

1. Get your team to tell you what skills are needed to support the services in your service catalogue.
2. Perform a morale baselining exercise within your team.
3. Try out brainstorming with Post-its© at your next team meeting.
4. Consider whether your existing organization structure is the right one for the future.

4 Project initiation

Once your business case has been approved there are a few tasks you need to do in order to set up the implementation project and establish the framework for the next few months. In addition to things you will need to do in each of the process areas, there are some general principles that you need to get in place early on or you may regret it later. The first is to confirm that your immediate manager is well aware of what you're doing and supports it wholeheartedly – ideally he or she will have been involved in the creation and submission of the business case. In any event, if you say you're starting a service improvement project then few managers will say that's a bad thing. Avoid using IT service management terminology that your manager may not be familiar with as this will only muddy the waters.

The next step is to try to clear the decks as much as possible by delaying anything that's non-essential and planning around critical projects that are dictated by the business (such as office moves). If you have a lot of these critical projects coming up then we would suggest you delay the service improvement until you have a better window of opportunity (although, of course, having better IT service management would help with the projects, so it's up to you).

Since this is a project it's a good idea to create a project initiation document (we've used the PRINCE2 term but this is often called 'Terms of Reference' or a variety of other names), based on the contents of the approved business case which sets out:

- who is going to do what (including who the project manager will be);
- what you think your organization will get out of it (benefits and objectives);
- the scope of your project;
- a rough timescale;
- the available budget;
- the resources allocated to the project;
- what could go wrong, and try to plan around it (project risk assessment);
- how often you're going to produce progress reports.

4   Project initiation

You then need to get this project initiation document agreed by the affected parties. It's a good idea to involve your team in the setting up of the project as this will help to gain their commitment to the road ahead – useful when the going gets tough.

Other essential tasks in the early days are as follows.

- Make a final decision on what training you are going to provide to what level and to whom, then get it booked. As we mentioned earlier there is a very well established set of training courses on ITIL V3 covering introductory through to expert levels and the range of ISO/IEC 20000 courses is also expanding to fill demand. Some of these courses (such as ITIL V3 Foundation) have exams associated with them and lead to the award of a qualification.
- Establish regular meetings and make sure they happen – a weekly management meeting of around an hour (if you have more than one manager/supervisor in the team) and a weekly team meeting of half to one hour to start off with. These meetings will be essential to communicate progress and obtain vital feedback from your team.
- Repeat your gap assessment on a quarterly basis or so to track progress and identify areas that are starting to lag behind.
- You should be able to prove that things are happening, so start to get in the habit of minuting meetings as soon as possible. This is a major culture change for many IT teams and an additional overhead – think about how to streamline it as much as you can, such as by just recording actions and decisions rather than lengthy narrative.

And if you have decided to go for certification to the ISO/IEC 20000 standard:

- Choose your auditors and get them in early on. A factor in the choice will be how does it fit in with any other quality accreditations you have (e.g. ISO 9001, ISO/IEC 27001) – if you have these it would make sense to use the same audit company.
- Book the audit date in plenty of time as the auditors tend to be very busy for months ahead. Be prepared to move it if progress is not as you hoped, but give them plenty of notice or you may end up still getting charged.

The first few weeks of an IT service management project are often the most crucial. By making sure you put in place the ideas proposed in this chapter, you can give your project the best chance of success and make the achievement of real benefits to users more likely.

4   Project initiation

Summary

- Commitment from your immediate manager is essential to the success of the project.
- It's a good idea to reduce the number of non-critical projects planned to happen at the same time as your IT service management implementation.
- A project initiation document sets out the scope, resources, budget and other attributes of the project from the outset, based on the agreed business case.
- Regular management and team meetings are essential to communicate progress, discuss issues and obtain feedback.
- If you have decided to go for certification to the ISO/IEC 20000 standard, choose your auditors and get them in early on.

Next steps

1. Raise the project at your next one-to-one meeting with your manager and confirm he or she is behind you.
2. Create a project initiation document and get it agreed.
3. Review the schedule of other projects for the next six to twelve months.
4. Schedule management and team meetings in the diary.

5 Implementing IT service management

Governance – the overall management system

In addition to the individual processes defined within good practice material, there is a need for an overall management system that directs, evaluates and improves how you perform IT service management within your organization. This is often referred to as 'governance' and it is a responsibility that falls necessarily to senior management. To use a nautical analogy, governance is about steering the right course whilst the engine room of IT service management processes produces the required power to turn the propeller. Many organizations establish a forum called an IT Steering Group, or similar, which consists of senior managers who meet on a regular basis to oversee the use and development of IT within the company. The focus of such groups is often weighted towards new projects but if you can convince it to address the management of existing services too, then this should be beneficial all round.

Management need to determine the fundamental objectives and policies for service management. Some of the initial round of this will have been done as part of the creation of a business case and Service Management Plan but there needs to be awareness of the fact that this will need to be monitored and amended to keep the aims of service management aligned with those of the overall business. How this is done, by whom and how frequently should be documented in the Service Management Policy so that everyone knows and understands their part in the IT service management system.

This part of ITSM can be seen, by some, as overly bureaucratic but it doesn't need to be. The ISO/IEC 20000 standard details what you need to be able to demonstrate is being done with regards to Governance and we'll give some brief and realistic guidance here. So before you plough headlong into designing your first process, it's a good idea to put some thought to your IT Service Management System, starting with the IT Service Management Policy.

Governance – the overall management system

The IT Service Management Policy

The IT Service Management Policy describes the overall approach that you have decided to take in the governance of IT service management within your organization. It documents how control will be exercised over the whole of ITSM and answers questions such as:

- How will processes be documented?
- How will improvements be assessed, authorized and monitored for effectiveness?
- How will process roles be assigned, defined and assessed?
- How will compliance be audited?
- How will risks and issues be logged, tracked and actioned?

To put it in quality management terms, this is your ITSM Quality Manual. In order to maintain control of the various processes and keep them all synchronized you will want to eliminate opportunities for confusion. To that end, you should ensure that the IT Service Management Policy defines processes and procedures appropriate to your organization's needs; if all processes are to be owned by a single person (as is common in very small teams) the elements of interaction between process owners may be a moot point, but in this case you will want to emphasize more fully the need for contingency arrangements and succession planning.

Common headings in an IT Service Management Policy include:

- Scope of IT service management;
- Overview of processes;
- High-level policy statements and objectives;
- Management of objectives and actions;
- Service management roles and responsibilities;
- Management of IT service management suppliers;
- Complaints and escalations;
- Interfaces with management and staff;
- Interfaces between processes;
- Interfaces with other functions (e.g. Project Office);
- Managing risks and issues;
- Resources, facilities, finances and budgets;
- Use of IT service management tools;
- Critical Success Factors and Key Performance Indicators;
- Audits;
- Management of improvements;
- Documentation management;
- Awareness and training.

Each of these areas needs to be thought through to set out how it will be handled within your organization; there is no 'one-size-fits-all' option here. As with all things in IT service management, these areas will evolve over time and you should include an explanation of how you will

5 Implementing IT service management

periodically re-evaluate and update all policies. We will cover some of the more important areas in the next few sections.

Service management roles and responsibilities

One of the first things that management needs to do is to establish the roles and responsibilities within the IT Service Management System. In a small team these will tend to fall to a select few people and in some cases it will all be down to one, but even if you are the sole role holder it helps to understand the different views you need to take on the services you provide and the processes that are used to provide them. There are a lot of roles defined in the ITIL V3 guidance (and we mean a lot) but there are some generic roles that we will outline here.

- Process Owner – the role responsible for ensuring the specific process is working as it should and that it is being improved over time; very much focused on the process itself.
- Service Owner – the role that takes a client-focused view of a single IT service that may use multiple processes in its execution.
- Process Manager – the role that actually manages the carrying out of the process on a day-to-day basis; for example, the Change Manager will handle the detail of change requests.

A useful way of documenting roles and responsibilities is in the form of a RACI chart where the tasks are listed down the left hand side, the roles are listed across the top and one or more letters (R for 'responsible', A for 'accountable', C for 'consulted' and I for 'informed') are inserted at the relevant intersection, as in the table below.

Table 1 – RACI chart

Task	Process owner	Service owner	Service manager	Change manager
Capture and record identified risks to processes	A/R	I	C/I	I
Approve major changes to process personnel		I	A/R	I
Update process documentation	A/R	C/I	C/I	I

Governance – the overall management system

The only specific rule with RACI charts is that only one role can be 'accountable' for the task.

The key point here is to define what should be done in each area and make sure that everyone in your team is aware of the part they have to play in the delivery of IT services.

Documentation management

Let's face it – no one likes doing documentation. It's one of those jobs that always gets pushed to the back of the list as soon as something more interesting comes along. If you're the only person that performs a task and you do it regularly then having it written down is of limited use to you. And therein lies the problem with getting people to document things – nine times out of ten it is of no use to them personally because they already know it. But it's very useful to the person who has to perform that task when the other person is on holiday, off sick or has left the company. To use an IT analogy to illustrate the point of how important documentation is, you wouldn't fail to back up your company's data because you know that if that server fails you could lose it all along with your job. Many of us have been through the situation where a problem with a tape drive or software has meant that backups are not happening, and had sleepless nights as a result. And yet we don't see the concept of backing up our IT staff knowledge in the same light, even though people are notoriously less reliable than any server.

So – at all levels from procedures up to processes, plans and strategies – documentation is absolutely key to delivering a good service and there is no point in having all those documents if you can't find them or if you don't know if you're using the latest version. This is where documentation management comes in; it doesn't have to be fancy but it does have to be clear.

You will need to think about where documentation will be stored; you don't necessarily need a single central store for all documents (indeed this is virtually impossible) but you should know what documentation you have and where it can be found, especially if you're thinking of actually going for certification. A simple register of what documentation and records exist should suffice including details of where they can be found, who owns them (perhaps a reference to the process owner), their purpose and how long they should be retained. There needs to be clear guidance about things like naming conventions, retention and disposal, and backups.

There are two main categories of documentation:
- records – which are defined by ISO as evidence of activities; and
- documents – which are defined as evidence of intention.

5   Implementing IT service management

So the procedure for logging an incident is a document as it shows how you intend to deal with a situation, whereas the incident itself is a record as it shows that and how action was taken.

You also need to think about the different forms that documentation can take. In the previous example the procedure could have been in paper form, an electronic document or perhaps HMTL. The incident record might conceivably be on paper but is more likely to be in an incident logging system, such as a spreadsheet or a database. All formats are acceptable but you need to be aware of how and where the information exists and how well it can be controlled.

Approvals and authorizations, as well as being needed as part of the processes themselves, are also needed in order to maintain governance. Can anyone change a process document or should it be approved at a certain level first? This point ties back to the earlier one about roles and responsibilities but now makes it real by asking you to explain how you will capture and record the authorizations to ensure that no new procedures are put in place without them having been signed off appropriately.

In order to keep track of different editions of the same document you will also need a simple form of version control. This will typically use a two-digit number such as 1.0 for the version followed by whether it is a final (i.e. approved) document or a draft. The version number will then be incremented according to the degree of change of the document – for example, for a significant rewrite the major number goes up (V1.0 becomes V2.0) or for a smaller change the minor number is incremented (V1.0 becomes V1.1). If you already have a convention within your organization it would make sense to use that rather than creating your own.

To finish off the rather dry but necessary subject of documentation, you will make your life much easier by making sure that each document also records the following items of information:

- author;
- owner (may be same as the author);
- date created;
- date approved;
- approved by;
- summary of changes from previous version;
- distribution (who is actually sent a copy).

If you decide to hold documents as configuration items and put amendments through your change management process then the change request number should also be recorded in the document.

Governance – the overall management system

Management review

A key part of the governance of the service management system is regular checking to see if all is running as it should. This involves scheduled reviews of all of the processes, using useful metrics to determine trends and areas that could be improved. For example, in change management are we getting an increase in emergency changes or failed changes? Is the number of incidents on an upward trend? Are configuration audits showing a lot of discrepancies? How often you perform such reviews depends upon your perception of how things are going; some organizations do them quarterly and in a stable situation every six months might be appropriate.

As well as process-specific reviews it's a good idea to hold a higher level review of the whole service management system at least once a year. This will involve discussions with customers to see whether their requirements have changed and what the impact of any changes will be. You will also want to assess whether the objectives set out in your Service Management Plan have been achieved and if not, why not? These kinds of assessment are best synchronized with the IT budget cycle as any changes may have financial implications for which you will need to have funds allocated.

Make sure you record the conclusions of each review and pass any actions across to your service improvement plan so that they don't get forgotten.

Internal and external audit

Your reviews will tell you a lot about how things are going but there really is no substitute for a good old-fashioned audit, whether it is internal or external. It's easy to convince yourself that all is well, particularly if you're very busy, but the relative formality of an audit will show up areas that you may have conveniently chosen to ignore. Internal auditors may use their own methods or could base the audit around COBIT or the ISO/IEC 20000 standard and, although it is hard to believe sometimes, they really are there to help you improve your service.

If you have an established internal audit department that will be your first port of call to arrange a programme of visits, but if not then third parties large and small are available to fill that gap. If your intention is to go for certification to the ISO/IEC 20000 standard then the audits will need to use this as their basis and we would suggest you start them sooner rather than later.

For more advice about external audits to the standard, please have a look at Chapter 7.

5   Implementing IT service management

Risk assessment

The assessment of risk is a common theme throughout this subject area and this book, and we discuss how to carry out a risk assessment for IT service continuity and for information security purposes in later sections. However, there are varying levels of risk assessment and at the level of the overall IT service management system there is also a need to think about what could go wrong and plan for it.

As with documentation standards, your organization may have a standard method of assessing risk at corporate level and it is worth understanding any existing methods in use and ensuring you are consistent with them. Within the Service Management Plan we will have defined our objectives for the coming year at least and planned our resources to achieve them. But things don't always go to plan so it is a good idea to sit down and consider what could happen that would affect the achievement of those objectives.

These will tend to be fairly high level such as:

- restriction of budget due to poor business environment;
- significant and unexpected business change, such as a merger or acquisition;
- loss of key resources (obviously this can have a major effect on a small team);
- major suppliers going into administration, or some form of dispute;
- regulatory or legislative changes;
- loss of senior management commitment, perhaps as a result of reorganization or promotion.

There will be others specific to your organization and industry that need to be considered and, for those that are above your risk threshold, you will need to either take some action now or plan a contingency if the risk becomes reality.

Summary

- Governance is about ensuring that the IT service management system is well defined and is delivering the required results.
- A key part of the overall governance is the definition of an IT Service Management Policy that sets out how the IT service management system functions in overview, including roles, processes, documentation and interfaces.
- Documentation management is an unpopular but necessary part of delivering effective IT service management.

- Regular management reviews, audits and risk assessments are essential to ensure you keep on track.

Next steps

1. Create a Service Management Policy covering the headings set out in this section.
2. Talk to other departments about what standards currently exist in your organization for things like risk assessment, documentation management and auditing.
3. Get some management reviews and audits booked in the diary.

The main points so far

We've covered a lot of ground in the preceding pages and at this stage it's probably worth pausing for a few moments to reiterate the main points so far before we continue into the specific processes of IT service management. The areas we have covered up to this point are concerned with setting the foundation and overall framework for the rest of the book in which we will explain how the individual processes will deliver results for you.

We started by setting out why we believe that IT service management is particularly important for a small IT team and how, in many ways, such a team is ideally placed to gain maximum benefit from the concepts developed by larger organizations. The overall goal is to move your team from being perceived as a necessary expense towards becoming a valued business partner, helping to drive the business forward and coming to be viewed as strategic asset that acts as a differentiator between your organization and the competition.

We then went on to tell you how IT service management is a discipline that is supported by a number of different frameworks, techniques and standards, each of which has its own merits, but that the main ones we would concentrate on are ITIL V3 and the ISO/IEC 20000 standard.

The next steps we recommended were to:

- conduct a gap analysis to assess how your current processes compare to the ISO/IEC 20000 standard;

5 Implementing IT service management

- baseline your current service so that you have a reliable foundation against which to measure your improvement initiatives;
- create a Service Management Plan setting out the approach you have chosen to take;
- formulate a business case to convince senior management that it's a good idea;
- consider your people issues so that your staff come with you rather than getting off at the first stop;
- initiate your project in a clear way, ensuring that the objectives are understood and deliverables defined;
- start to form your service management system to provide overall governance around your processes so that they can be continuously measured and improved.

We remind you of these points because we know it's very easy to become engrossed in the mechanics of a specific process and temporarily lose sight of the bigger picture. Try to ensure that you have the above areas covered before looking to change the way you do things; as in all project management up-front planning can prevent uncertainty and confusion later on.

Of course, in our earlier section 'How to use this book' we did say that an alternative approach is to adopt a low key bottom-up method, improving individual processes as you see fit and using resource when it is available – and we stand by this assertion. Sometimes there just isn't the appetite amongst senior management for this kind of project and it would be a pity to do nothing. If you do decide to take this approach we would still recommend baselining each process before you start and making sure the people issues are considered. Once you have become more comfortable with the concepts you may feel it is worth a try with senior management on a more formal footing, particularly if some budget is needed to progress further.

Having run over the main points in summary, it's time to get into some process detail.

Resolution processes

And so we come to the implementation, or more likely improvement, of the resolution processes, incident management and problem management. These are key to the provision of an effective front-line service to the user and warrant a significant amount of time to be spent on them to get them right and then keep them under review.

Resolution processes

Incident management

Objective

To restore agreed service to the business as soon as possible or to respond to service requests.

An incident is commonly defined as 'any event that is not part of the standard operation of a service and that causes, or may cause, an interruption to, or a reduction in, the quality of service'.

So, what does that mean? Well, in simple terms it's when something goes wrong (or is about to go wrong) and that impacts the user's ability to use the service. Examples might include a PC not working, a network connection down (which might obviously affect multiple users) or, as an example of something that is about to go wrong, the server disk is at 95 per cent full.

The aim of incident management is to restore normal service (or avoid the loss of service) as quickly as possible with little regard as to why the issue happened in the first place. This process is very focused on the Service Level Agreement targets that promise maximum levels of downtime, so the quicker the user(s) can be restored to being fully operational, the better.

There are various teams involved in incident management as, in reality, this process forms a large part of what most IT departments spend their time doing. The first team to get involved is the service desk. Now, this sounds quite grandiose and large, but in reality it need consist of nothing more than a person on the end of a phone (or other communication method such as email) with the ability to log the call, offer some initial (possibly even scripted) support and give feedback to users as to the status of their calls. This includes incidents, chases and service requests. We'll cover the activities of the service desk more fully in a little while, but it's worth saying here that the detail of what the service desk does and how it works should be documented in a policy statement that can inform the rest of the incident management process.

The next team to get involved will generally be the technical teams, sometimes referred to as the 'resolver' teams for obvious reasons. These will be the teams (or individuals) within IT with responsibility for the various systems and applications. For example, you may have a team responsible for database maintenance or network infrastructure; in a small IT team this may be the same person but it is worth considering naming these roles even if they are then assigned to the same individual as, you never know, your team may grow and when it does you have already built your organization structure, and your processes reflect that structure.

5 Implementing IT service management

Possibly the most important player in all of this is the user. ITSM distinguishes between a user and a customer by saying that the customer is the individual who defines, agrees and pays for the service whereas a user merely uses it. Obviously a customer can also be a user but they do not necessarily have to be the same. There are other players who may get involved in, or provide support to, incident management such as the Problem Manager and Change Manager.

The life cycle of an incident

There are several stages in the life cycle of an incident and you should consider carefully how you process and record each stage as, don't forget, this process is one of the main interfaces with the users. Failing on this one will have a far greater effect on user and customer perception and satisfaction than many of the other processes.

The full incident process is shown in Figure 4. The main steps are as follows.

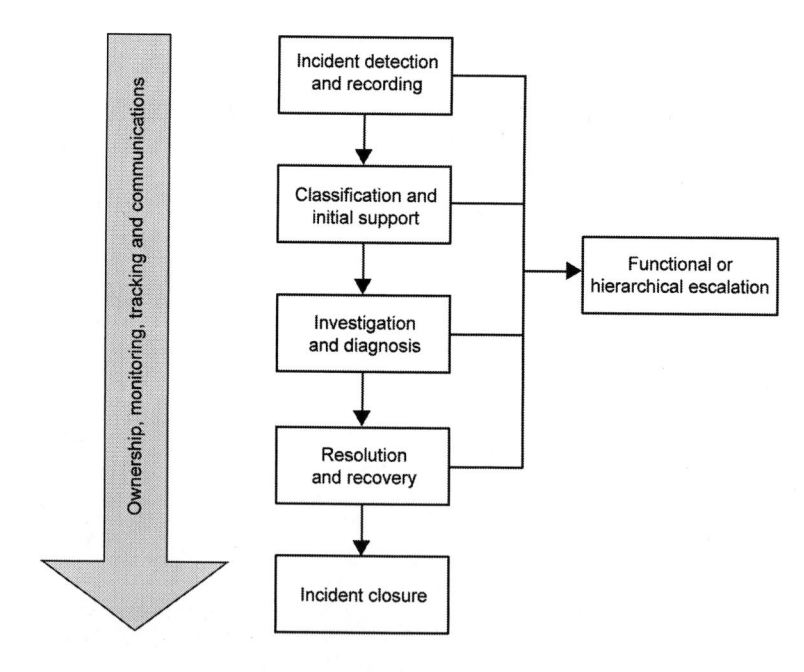

Figure 4 – Typical incident management process flow

Resolution processes

Incident detection and recording

Okay, so the user's PC has failed; in reality the incident has begun but, until you are aware of it, you can't be working to rectify it; so the first step is detection. This could be through automation; event management systems are available that will raise an incident when a certain pre-agreed condition occurs – perhaps a server crashes – or it could be through the user calling or emailing the service desk.

Obviously the next step is to record the incident. There is a huge variety of systems on the market for incident recording from small to large scale, locally hosted or SaaS (Software as a Service) but the essential operation at this stage is to capture the basic information: user details (name, location, contact number/email), fault description, time of occurrence and time of logging. As long as you have a system capable of recording these details and providing a unique call reference number, you're in business. This could be something as simple as an Excel spreadsheet but we wouldn't advise that: as the call goes on, there will be more information recorded and a spreadsheet would quickly become unwieldy and impractical.

Classification and initial support

The next thing that needs to be done is to classify the incident. Classifying is actually two things: prioritizing and categorizing – both are essential for the correct routing, diagnosis and eventual resolution of the incident and care should be taken to set up the priorities and categories correctly for your organization.

It might be that you only need three levels of priority – High, Medium and Low – but even then you need to be very clear about what you mean by each of these terms. You might define High to mean that more than 50 per cent of your user base is affected (unable to use the service), but would that account for the time when your five users in payroll are unable to access the payroll system on the 29th of the month? Make sure that your priorities and definitions are clear and well communicated; it will help to avoid confusion and conflict – we're all probably well aware of situations that warranted a High priority and were not well catered for in the priority definition.

Similarly you need to give some thought to the categories you want to have available. Many systems allow various levels of category so you might have the sort of list shown in Figure 5.

IT Service Management for Small IT Teams

5   Implementing IT service management

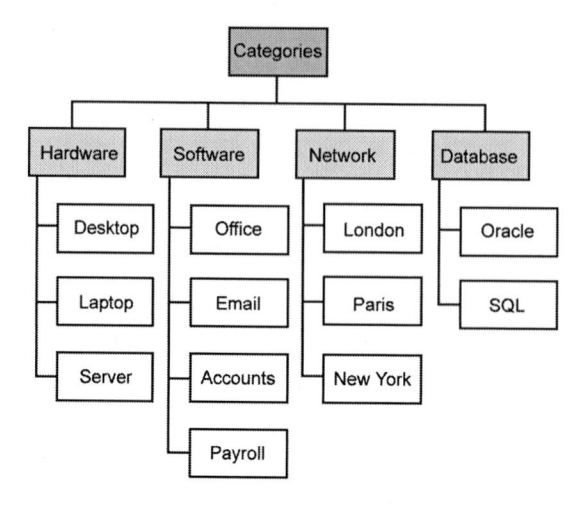

Figure 5 – Simple incident management category tree

Of course, this is a very simplistic example but you get the idea. As with priorities, make the categories relevant for your organization and, above all else, clear and unambiguous. This information can be hugely useful as, in the immediate term, it can determine to which team (or individual) you should route this incident and, in the longer term, it can help you to identify troublesome systems or components (more of this in the section headed 'Problem management'.

The second part of this stage is 'initial support'. This incident may be one that has happened before, so it's worth looking it up in your knowledge base if you have one or simply searching the incident database for similar incidents. if they are in the same room ask your colleagues, and perhaps use some standard techniques to resolve this – remember the aim of incident management is to restore normal service as quickly as possible so, if all it takes is 'have you tried switching it off and on again?', then so be it. We'll worry about why it happened in the first place later but for now 'Hooray!', the user is back up and working, you can move on to incident closure. However, if the quick fixes haven't done the trick then you need to move on to the next stage.

Resolution processes

Case in point

> The IT Manager had agreed the SLA for incidents with the business and communicated this to his staff. This worked well until the Chief Executive wanted his BlackBerry fixed immediately, despite the fact that it was on a two-day SLA. After initially sticking to the agreed timescales, the help desk was ordered to drop everything, including more urgent work, to get the job done straight away. After this a specific SLA exception was agreed with the executive team and they were defined as VIPs within the service desk system.

One point to note here is that you should also give some thought to how long you would want the service desk (or whoever is tasked with the initial support activity) to spend on this. They need to spend sufficient time that a large proportion of the incidents are fixed quickly at the first point of contact – i.e. the user's incident is resolved before he or she even puts the phone down. But the longer the service desk spends on an incident that they cannot resolve the less time the subsequent teams have to spend on it – remember we're against the SLA clock on incidents. Also, if you're talking about a single person service desk then all the time that person is on the phone to this user trying to do initial support there may be other users who can't get through to log their incidents. This has several implications: there may be a trend building up that you are not aware of as you're not hearing about the incidents as quickly as you should, the users will perceive IT to be unable to deal with their calls and, as pointed out before, it forms a bottleneck meaning that the service desk is the only part of IT that is dealing with incidents.

Diagnosis

Okay, so the initial support didn't resolve the user's incident, but at least you now know what you're dealing with, the priority and, potentially, what steps didn't work. Now it's time to pass the call (ITIL calls this 'escalation') to the appropriate technical team. Hopefully the categorization should give you a really good steer on which team this needs to go to; if not, you might need to do some further investigation.

The technical team will, as this stage suggests, do some further investigation and hopefully diagnose the cause. Once they have a cause and a proposed resolution the incident moves on to the next stage. If, after deeper investigation, the technical team is still unable to determine the cause, it may be necessary to raise a problem record.

5 Implementing IT service management

We'll deal with problem management more fully in the next section but at this stage it is sufficient for us to say that a problem is the unknown, underlying cause of one or more incidents.

Resolution

So, after perhaps a lot of head-scratching and investigation, you work out what needs to be done to get things working properly again. Resolution is about restoring service to the user. Some resolutions may be simple (rebooting a PC); others may require replacement of hardware or software or a combination of the two. Once you have effected a resolution, there may be recovery actions that need to be performed to get the user back to fully operational. For instance, if the resolution required replacement of a server hard disk, generally you will also need to re-image, reinstall or restore a backup before the hard disk is useable and the overall service is recovered. Sometimes you will be able to resolve a user's incident without finding out what caused it and, in incident management terms, this is acceptable – they are working again and it's smiles all round. However, you know at the back of your mind that, since you don't know the cause, this could happen again. So what do you do? This is where incident management interfaces with problem management to put a marker down to say that we need to come back to this incident and work out why it happened. The incident is closed, but a problem is opened.

Incident closure

After all the work has been done, the incident has been resolved and the service has been recovered, that's it right? You can close the incident and move on, yes? Well, almost. Since this is IT service management and the correct operation of the service is as viewed from the user's perspective, you need to get their confirmation before you can close the incident. Some organizations make it a policy to obtain positive confirmation from the user before closing all incidents. However, this often leads to incidents staying open for prolonged periods as the user, perhaps rightly, sees that their service is now running and doesn't much care about closing your incident record. Other organizations take the approach that there will be a cut-off time after which, if no reply has been received from the user, the incident will be automatically closed. You need to define the appropriate policy for your organization and get it agreed and communicated.

Escalation

There are two sorts of escalation: functional and hierarchic. Functional escalation deals with the transfer of an incident between functional teams (for example, from the web team to the network team) whereas hierarchic escalation deals with what is normally understood by escalation – raising the incident to progressively higher levels of management. How, when and to whom incidents should be escalated should be defined, agreed and communicated through the incident management policy. Incident management tools will often automate this process for you.

Ownership, monitoring, tracking and communication

Concurrent with all of the above stages, you (or someone to whom you have delegated the task) should be monitoring the progress of the resolution of the incident and keeping those who are affected by the incident up to date with the status. This is often handled by the service desk but, in small teams, you may assign an individual to just keep an eye on the queue of incidents and perhaps prod individuals from time to time. This role would be referred to as the Incident Manager.

The incident management policy

Some of the considerations for your incident management policy have been mentioned as we've been going through, but here is a more consolidated list:

1. *Sources* – What sources will you accept for incidents to be logged? Phone calls? Email? Walk-ins? Self-service? Do you have a preferred source that you will encourage users to use and, if so, which?
2. *Priorities* – How many levels of priority will you use and what will they mean?
3. *Timescales* – You need to give some thought to how long you will allow for each of the stages in the incident process. The timescale will need to reflect the priority accorded the incident and the SLA for the service.
4. *Roles and responsibilities* – Who is involved in the process and what is their role in it?
5. *Escalation* – How, when and to whom will calls be escalated? This should be done with an eye to service level targets – it's best to escalate the matter before it breaches its target. Regarding functional escalation, the policy should detail which teams are involved and how hand-off will be performed – i.e. will there be an acknowledgement sent when the receiving team accepts the incident or will it be taken on faith that they've seen it and are working on

5 Implementing IT service management

it? (Tip: if you don't want calls breaching targets left, right and centre, don't assume that people are working on it; include a step which verifies the fact.)

6. *Incident closure* – How will you verify the user's acceptance of an incident closure? How long will you wait? Will a verbal acceptance be sufficient or do you need an email?
7. *Interfaces* – Think about how your process will interact with other IT service management and other business processes; problem management, change management and configuration management are the obvious ones but you should also think about how you can inform capacity management when there are performance issues, how availability management can use your data to analyse service availability and what interaction needs to take place between incident management and service level management in order to ensure that incident resolution targets are delivered.
8. *Reopening* – Will you allow incidents to be reopened? If so, who can authorize and under what conditions?
Some organizations operate a policy that if the reopen request occurs within 24 hours of the call closure, it is allowed and can be performed by the service desk operative; after that a new call must be logged.
9. *Major incidents* – Define what you and the business consider to be a major incident and what that will mean in terms of resources, prioritization and the major incident process itself.
10. *Information* – Give some thought to what information you need to collect/record about the incident. This will be driven to some extent by the process itself, but you may have other information specific to your organization which will help with resolution or with subsequent analysis.
11. *Post incident reviews* – Will you undertake PIRs for all incidents (not recommended) or for those meeting certain criteria (perhaps only Priority One calls)?
12. *Communications and reporting* – Think about what communications will take place during and after incidents and what information will be communicated and reported on an ongoing basis.
13. *Metrics* – You should define metrics that you can use to monitor the day-to-day effectiveness and efficiency of the process. Key metrics you should consider are:
    - total number of incidents broken into the various stages (logged, undergoing diagnosis, closed, etc.);
    - number (and percentage) of major incidents;
    - mean elapsed time to achieve incident resolution;
    - number (and percentage) of incidents incorrectly assigned or incorrectly categorized;
    - number (and percentage) of incidents reopened;
    - number of incidents closed by the first point of contact (usually the service desk).

Resolution processes

Summary

- Incident management is a key ITSM process to get right as it is very visible to the user and can have a significant effect on business productivity.
- The incident management process is about getting the user working again as soon as possible rather than necessarily finding out what went wrong (this is the purpose of problem management).
- The service desk carries out the incident management process assisted, where required, by resolver groups.
- Significant thought needs to be put into the definition of an incident management policy – including priorities, categories, escalation and closure.

Next steps

1. Determine a policy for how incidents will be managed.
2. Identify opportunities for automating the incident logging process.
3. Agree, with the business, the priorities and categories to be used, and what they mean.
4. Create a policy to govern how much time should be spent by each team at each stage.
5. Define how the process will interface with other processes such as problem management, change management, information security management.

Problem management

Objective

To minimize disruption to the business by proactive identification and analysis of the cause of incidents and by managing problems to closure.

Problem management is a huge boon to a small IT team since the whole aim is to reduce the reactive workload which is the bane of all IT teams but which impacts on small teams worse than most. But what do we mean by a 'problem'? A problem is defined by ITIL® as 'the unknown cause of one or more incidents'.

5 Implementing IT service management

Let's give you an example: A user logs an incident that jobs are being sent to the printer but nothing is coming out. After checking the usual (Switched on? Plugged in? Right printer?), the service desk analyst suggests that the user reboots his or her PC and, hey presto, 15 copies of the user's report start spewing from the printer. Incident closed. The following day, the same user calls up with the same issue. A different service desk analyst picks up this call and (tut, tut) doesn't check for prior incidents but gets the user to reboot the PC. Surprise, surprise – same result, printer now works. Incident closed. This happens repeatedly over the next two days. Is this an efficient way of doing things? No! What you need here is problem management. The idea is to get to the bottom of why things go wrong in the first place, rather than cleaning up time and time again afterwards. It's one of those jobs that you know you should do, but you just never seem to get around to. If you make that extra effort, it will make life so much easier.

Case in point

> After the first incident was logged a flurry of further calls were received by the service desk. File serving was very slow and users were getting frustrated, although rebooting the PC seemed to help. A problem record was opened and an investigation was begun. Was it the replication software, or the lack of disk arms on the server, or some essential profile moves that were being carried out that was causing the problem? Over a period of weeks a series of changes were implemented to try to relieve the issue with no success. The hardware supplier was called in to size new servers and purchase or loan alternatives were costed. Eventually, after several weeks, an overnight disk defrag resolved the problem. A major problem review was held and a number of lessons learned.

Problem management should really kick-in at the point where the first incident was logged as there was an issue of unknown cause, but generally your policy would err away from logging every incident as a problem. Instead it might state that on the second occurrence of the same incident, whilst at the same time resolving the incident, the operator should open a linked problem record for someone to follow up and try to identify the underlying cause. This is termed 'reactive problem management' for obvious reasons.

Problem management can also start off with all incident history and seek to identify trends which perhaps weren't spotted as they didn't initially

Resolution processes

seem related – perhaps a user login issue and a printer spooling issue which, although they don't appear to be related, might share a common factor such as the server being used. This might lead to an investigation of that server revealing memory or disk space issues; this is 'proactive problem management'.

A third thread of problem management works very closely with availability and capacity management to identify areas where the very fabric of the IT infrastructure may, in the future, lead to an increased number of incidents. Problem management would then seek to raise changes to alleviate or avoid the situation – a kind of 'preventative' method.

In a small IT team the people involved are likely to be the same players as in incident management: the service desk will play a large part in capturing and identifying problems; the same resolver teams are likely to be involved in investigating the root causes. Unlike incident management, users are not usually so involved in problem management as their primary concern should be getting back up and running ... which is handled by incident management. Your average user doesn't care much why it happened just so long as (a) it's fixed, (b) it doesn't happen again, and (c) if it does, you're working on ways to get it fixed again more quickly. So they might be interested to know that you're working towards stopping it happening again and reducing the impact to them but apart from that, they don't care too much. Your resolver teams may also have to interact with them to get more information. Customers will want to know about how you are going about the process of reducing the number of outages and incidents to their services as it directly affects the level of service you deliver and the level of customer satisfaction which you maintain. So you will want to keep them informed on a regular basis.

Ideally there will be a small function with responsibility for problem management specifically. It is usually quoted as a good idea to make it independent of the incident management function as there are sometimes conflicting demands – incident management want the issue resolved and the user returned to normal service ASAP; problem management might need to keep the users off the server for a little while longer to check a few more things. But if you don't have the staff numbers for this don't worry too much – most IT professionals are capable of balancing the demands of resolution time against investigation time and this should be well documented in the incident and problem management policies anyway.

Again, as with incident management, there are many other players who get involved: change management for handling changes raised to resolve problems, configuration management for providing detailed analysis of the infrastructure to assist with trending and, as stated earlier, availability and capacity management are closely linked with problem management.

5 Implementing IT service management

The life cycle of a problem

Like an incident, a problem is managed via a process and it helps if you have a good tool to support this. There should certainly be a system for recording and tracking problems and, because of the strong linkage with incident management, it is usually recommended that they share a common tool with the ability to handle and link both. However, the main requirement is for tools and data to allow the analysis of incident data for trending and root cause analysis. The problem records themselves, at a basic level, are merely a list of named issues, with dates and linked incident information. In the same way as an incident management policy is useful, it is a good idea to create a problem management policy document which sets out clearly how this area is approached within your organization. The headings for this will be broadly the same as those outlined in the last section on incident management.

A typical problem management process is shown in Figure 6.

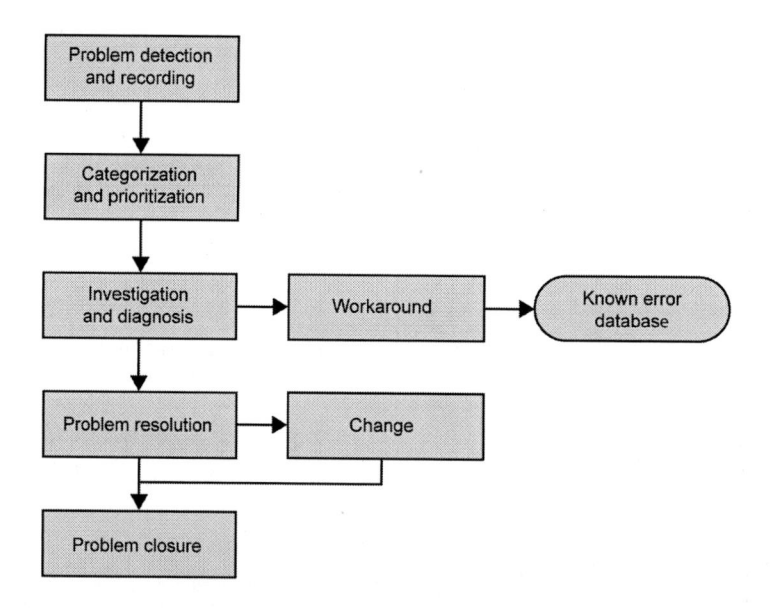

Figure 6 – Typical problem management process

We will now look at the main steps in this process.

Resolution processes

Detect and record

A problem can be identified from a number of sources:

- the service desk may identify that there may be an unknown cause behind one or more incidents;
- a technical team may, upon analysis of an incident assigned to it, determine that the cause is unknown;
- a supplier may notify you that a problem exists and is being worked on – for example, security vulnerability reports where a workaround is given and an ETA for a full fix is provided would be classed as a problem;
- proactive problem management may, through analysis of historic incident data, identify a common, though still unknown, thread behind multiple incidents;
- release management may highlight pre-existing known errors in software being released from development; software is often released with known 'bugs' which have been accepted as permissible by the customer.

Once detected, a problem record should be created to act as a place to log the details of the problem and its progress and permit future analysis.

Classify

The problem should then be assigned a category. It is advisable to use a consistent categorization coding between incident management and problem management to enable easier analysis and traceability.

In the same way that incidents must be prioritized, all problems must be too. You can use the same principles for prioritizing problems as you do for incidents, but be careful to define the appropriate targets for resolution separately (if you decide to do this – some IT teams do not specify resolution targets for problems as they are by their very nature an unknown quantity).

As well as impact to the business, it is also recommended that the prioritization of problems takes into account the impact to IT resources – how much resource will it take to recover? With what skill levels? How much will it cost? etc.

Diagnosis

This is where the sleuthing begins – using a number of techniques (which are outside the scope of this book, but you may wish to look up Chronological Analysis, Kepner and Tregoe and Ishikawa Diagrams in the appendices of the *ITIL V3 Service Operation Guide*) the technical teams attempt to ascertain the underlying cause of the problem. This may involve reviewing logs, running diagnostic tools and talking to users to

5   Implementing IT service management

obtain more information about when, how and where the relevant incidents occurred – are there any discernible patterns?

Workarounds and known errors

It is often possible to find a workaround that will either temporarily ease the underlying cause resulting in fewer incidents or will permit a fast restoration of service to those still affected by it. This does not mean that the problem is resolved and can be closed, nor does it mean that ongoing work to discover the cure should be halted. It merely means that users can get back to their work – the service desk should be informed whenever a workaround is identified.

An example might be to perform a nightly reboot of a server which is suffering from memory leakage while the technical team continue to try to ascertain which program is faulty. The result is that the users remain unaffected during the day but the cause and final cure have not yet been determined.

As soon as a cure or a workaround is identified, this should be entered as a known error in the known error database (KEDB). Incident management teams should refer to the KEDB when they are attempting to resolve an incident to ascertain if it is as a result of a pre-existing problem and if there is already a cure or workaround available.

Resolve

Once the underlying cause is known and a fix has been identified, it may be applied in order to resolve the problem. This should be performed under the control of change management to ensure that any risks are assessed. There are occasions where the solution discovered cannot be justified – for example, where the impact is small but the cost of the solution is high. The business may take the decision to not implement the solution and continue to rely on the workaround. In such cases the problem record should be flagged to ensure that ongoing work on the solution ceases but that the problem is henceforth excluded from team performance metrics; otherwise it will start to look like the team assigned the problem is taking an age to implement the solution. These flagged records should be evaluated periodically to determine whether technology or circumstances have changed sufficiently to require the reassessment of the solutions justification.

Closure

When any required changes have been successfully made to resolve the problem it should be closed. This may also trigger the closure of associated incident records which remain open and the associated user verification of those closures. At this point any known error records should also be updated. It is recommended that the problem record be

Resolution processes

reviewed at closure to make sure that all of the information has been recorded clearly so as to permit future analysis.

Major problem review

In the same way that there should be a definition in the incident management policy for what the organization deems a major incident, there should be a definition in the problem management policy for a 'major' problem.

Upon closure of a problem deemed to be major, a review should take place to examine:

- what was done well;
- what could have been done better;
- how to prevent recurrence;
- whether there was any third party responsible;
- whether follow-up actions are needed.

Any actions arising should be added to your service improvement plan so that they are visible and can be addressed.

Summary

- Problem management is a huge boon to a small IT team since the whole aim is to reduce the reactive workload which is the bane of all IT teams but which impacts on small ones worse than most.
- A problem is defined by ITIL as 'the unknown cause of one or more incidents'. A known error is a problem that has been diagnosed successfully (or has a workaround) but is not yet fixed.
- A problem management policy details the ways in which problems can be detected and logged, what information needs to be collected and recorded, the roles and responsibilities of those involved, how information about problems will be disseminated and shared among the technical groups, what techniques will be used for diagnosis, etc.
- In the same way that all incidents must be logged even if they have already been resolved, all problems must be logged. This ensures that the historic data reflects a true position and can be used for trending and analysis.

5   Implementing IT service management

Next steps

> 1. Look at your existing service desk tool to see how it may be able to log problems as well as incidents.
> 2. Define your problem management policy and process.
> 3. Start to log problems and diagnose their root cause.

Other ITIL service operation processes

Although the 2005 version of the ISO/IEC 20000 standard defines only two resolution processes, ITIL V3 goes a bit further and describes three further processes that may be of use to a small IT team, and we will briefly cover them here. They are request fulfilment, event management and access management.

Request fulfilment

Like incident management, request fulfilment is a process you are almost certainly doing already as it is, by its nature, essential to the operation of a service desk. Good practice recommends the separation of incidents and service requests because they are different in a number of ways. First and foremost, whilst an incident is a report of something broken, a service request is a report of something that the user wants. Typical examples of service requests include:

- a new user to be created;
- some equipment to be purchased;
- a desk and associated kit to be moved;
- clarification on service desk opening times;
- how to use a feature of an application;
- a complaint (or compliment) about a service or member of staff.

The first three of these examples are, in fact, standard changes – predefined, low risk changes that don't need to go through the full change management process. Such standard changes are requested via the service desk as a service request and many organizations will look to automate as much of the processing of these requests as possible. The ideal will be to provide a self-service portal to the user which captures the required information and routes it directly to the person who needs to approve the request, if necessary bypassing the service desk. Although such self-service portals can be difficult to create they have the potential to positively affect the workload of the service desk and so should be seriously looked at.

Resolution processes

Service requests are also different from incidents in that they will usually have longer timescales associated with them as they are usually less urgent and may rely upon an external supplier, for example, for equipment requests. These timescales should be agreed with the business as part of your SLA – although for requests such as new user set-up customers rarely seem to plan ahead, often informing the service desk on the Friday of a new starter on the Monday. Remember, however, that if a one-day turnaround is what the business really needs and it is willing to pay for the IT team to be resourced accordingly, then this may be perfectly appropriate.

Event management

Also new with ITIL V3 was the process of event management. In practice this involves monitoring the IT estate, using one or more software tools, and then having the correct procedures in place to react to events that occur that have some kind of significance – usually that something has happened or is about to happen. Examples would be a server failing or disk usage passing a threshold value. The trick once an exception event (i.e. one we need to do something about) is detected is to ensure that it goes through the correct IT service management process; this could be incident, problem or change management. Most monitoring tools can produce an email alert which can be sent to an inbox that is watched by your service desk tool and an incident automatically created. Whilst this can be very useful, you will need to avoid the situation where many erroneous incidents are automatically generated, so some experimentation will be called for here.

Access management

This process deals with the management of user accounts and permissions according to the information security policy. Most such activities will be handled via the request fulfilment process above (e.g. new user creation). A key step is the confirmation of identity to ensure that the people making requests are who they say they are, especially if contacting the service desk via phone. This is an area often neglected in a small IT team, partly because the staff on the service desk may know the majority of the users and recognize their voices.

The remainder of this area is concerned with creating groups for users, so that access rights are inherited in the correct way, and regularly reviewing the degree of access in place. Most organizations attempt to liaise with HR to keep on top of starters and leavers, with varying results. This is a good idea if your HR team is willing to play and can provide the information regularly and in a useable format. This area should also be

5 Implementing IT service management

heavily involved in the development and release of new services to ensure the integrity of the security of the live environment.

Summary

- Request fulfilment is well worth spending some time on to analyse and automate as much as possible.
- Event management can help you to identify incidents before, or as soon as, they happen and take appropriate action.
- Access management deals with the way in which users are created and permissions assigned.

Next steps

1. Create a list of your common requests and see to what extent they could be automated.
2. Review your use of monitoring tools to see how they could be used to spot incidents before they happen.
3. Check that your service desk confirms the identity of users requesting access to systems in an appropriate way.

Control processes

The control processes, change, release and configuration management provide a solid framework to protect the integrity of your live environment and give you a fuller understanding of how your IT estate fits together.

Change management

Objective

To ensure all changes are assessed, approved, implemented and reviewed in a controlled manner.

Once your IT services are in place they should, in theory at least, keep running with a minimum of outside intervention. This is true of processes performed by people just as it is of data processed by hardware and

Control processes

software. Yes, hardware breaks and accidents happen but, generally, if you leave it alone very little should go wrong. Until you start to change it.

Change is often quoted as being one of the few certainties in life; nothing stays the same forever. Managed change can certainly be a very good thing, leading to improvements for the future and taking the organization forward. If an organization wishes to stay in business in an often competitive market, then it has to change with the times and that means changing its IT systems too. But with change inevitably comes risk and the potential to bring down previously serviceable systems that are essential to the day-to-day workings of the organization. This is where the process of change management comes in. This process is all about protecting the live environment but, at the same time, allowing beneficial change to take place in as low risk a fashion as possible, and without introducing an administrative nightmare that leads to IT staff circumventing the process when they can.

So do you know what changes are happening to the services you support? The chances are that if you don't have change management in place then you don't; you may be aware of some or even many of them, but certainly not all. And that means you have a risk that is currently unquantified and unmanaged.

This risk may be due to a number of reasons, such as:

- changes are poorly thought through and so don't have the effect that was intended;
- they are implemented without considering their impact on users;
- the reason for doing the change is not clear and the cost may not be justified;
- the actions required if the change goes wrong are not considered;
- changes are not tested properly before or after implementation;
- more than one person may be changing the same item, each not knowing about the other.

These risks can cause major problems even in a small IT team where communication is generally good. And it's often not the person that made the unsuccessful change that feels the pain afterwards; unless he or she is also on first-line service desk. Change management is all about managing the risk of change. It does not remove the risk completely; changes will still fail even after you have put a process in place, but hopefully less often and they will have less of an impact on users.

There are a number of steps you will need to take to get basic change management in place in your IT team. We'll go through them and explain the essentials before talking about release management, which is a related process that deals with the roll-out of a number of related changes that have a wider than normal impact.

5 Implementing IT service management

In a small IT team the allocation of roles is usually fairly straightforward as the choice is somewhat limited. Often the IT Manager will take the role of Change Manager, who is responsible for the process overall and running the Change Advisory Board meetings (see the next section, 'Change management process'). If you have the resources you may also decide to appoint a Change Co-ordinator who will do some of the administration of the process, but a goal should be to minimize this admin as much as possible.

In order to make sure that everyone logs changes and follows the new process, you will need to be clear about what it covers, at least in the first phase. For example, do you want to manage changes to software applications or restrict the scope to servers and network infrastructure? You will also have a number of common changes that happen all the time – for example, new user creations, PC installations or individual file restores. You probably don't want to take these types of small, low-risk change through a full change management process as it would delay them unnecessarily and be of little benefit. So these are usually managed as a separate kind of change known as the 'service request' and are logged and processed on the service desk system as such. Create yourself a list of these service requests and make it clear to your team that these don't need to be logged as change requests (but they still need to be recorded).

Change management process

Now you'll need to define a process so that everyone in your team knows what they should be doing. A simple flowchart will suffice at first, such as the one shown in Figure 7, and this can be developed as the process beds in and lessons are learned from the experience of running it. The following are the main points that need to be covered in the process.

Log changes as change requests

This is probably the most difficult, but at the same time most important, part of introducing change management – getting staff to log changes in the first place. The key point to make to your IT staff when introducing change management is that logging a change request and getting it authorized provides them with additional protection in the event that it goes wrong. If someone else has confirmed the need for it, checked the plan and agreed the timing, then it's unrealistic for the implementer to take all the blame for a failed change. The cause probably lies somewhere in the change management process and can be addressed as an improvement so that it is less likely to happen again. In the first few weeks, however, you will need to be vigilant to ensure that changes are not being made outside of the process and you may need to clarify what is and isn't within scope.

Control processes

Change requests are often logged on the same service desk system as that used for incident and problem management and this is useful because you will be able to link the different types of records together to provide an audit trail. But if your system does not support change management then a spreadsheet approach, perhaps combined with document templates for change request forms, is perfectly workable at first.

There are a number of basic details that need to be included on the change request:

- Who is submitting it?
- Description of the change – what needs to be done?
- Business reason for the change – why does it need to happen?
- Testing to be carried out before the change (to check that it will work) and after the change (to check it has indeed worked).
- Backout plan – what will we do if the change has unexpected results and we want to remove it again?
- Anticipated date for the change to happen.

The Change Manager should perform an initial check of the details supplied when the request is logged to make sure all the required information has been provided to a sufficient level of detail to allow assessment to take place.

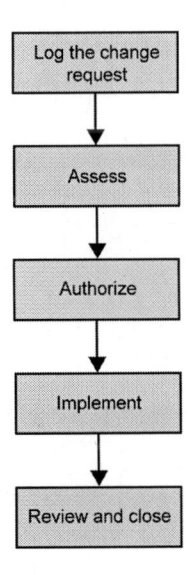

Figure 7 – Basic change management process

IT Service Management for Small IT Teams

5   Implementing IT service management

Assess the change request

There is little point in getting IT staff to log change requests if they then have to wait too long for them to be assessed and hopefully authorized. If this is the case there is a danger that the process will fall into disuse as staff will not see the point in logging them in the first place. The Change Advisory Board (CAB) is a rather old-fashioned name for a meeting where changes are assessed on a regular basis, led by the Change Manager. A reasonable minimum frequency is probably once a week for a small IT team but this will, of course, depend upon the number of changes to be assessed. The attendees just need to be the people with an interest in one or more of the changes being reviewed and you may decide to bring people in only at the times when their changes are being assessed in order to make best use of their valuable time. In a small team the point is often made that only one person has the technical knowledge to know whether the proposed change will work, and that person is the one who raised the change in the first place. The benefit of using the change management process in these cases is in the structured questioning of the technician so that he or she is confident that it has been tested it and knows what to do if it doesn't work; these are still valid points even if the technicalities are not understood by the Change Manager.

As with most of the processes of IT service management, it's a good idea to make the CAB meetings as short and to the point as possible with a minimum of admin afterwards. To this end we would recommend that you conduct the meeting with the change management system on a screen or projector and update it directly during the meeting.

As Change Manager you may decide to assess and authorize some smaller changes prior to the next CAB meeting, particularly if it is a few days away. This is perfectly acceptable as long as all of the areas listed in the next paragraph are addressed during the assessment. Waving change through without backout or test plans is a bad idea and will undo all your good work in implementing change management.

Newly logged changes will need to be assessed in a number of ways to satisfy the Change Manager that they are suitable to proceed. The main areas for assessment are as follows.

- *Completeness* – Has the submitter provided all the required information? Often aspects such as testing and backout plans are neglected; if they are not up to scratch the Change Manager should refer the change request back to the submitter to do it properly.
- *Business justification* – Is the change worth the time and money it will cost to implement?
- *Risk* – How likely is the change to succeed? Has it been tested and planned adequately? Has the person who will implement it enough knowledge and experience to make it work? Watch out for changes that can't be backed out.

Control processes

- *Timing* – When is the best time to implement it? What periods should be avoided, for example, during year-end processing or Christmas for a retailer?
- *Security, capacity and service continuity* – Does the change affect any of these areas, for example, a server location move may mean that the service continuity plan needs to be amended too?

This sounds like a lot to look at, but as you get used to the process it will become second-nature to think about each of these areas. As part of the assessment of the change you will also need to classify it according to a simple scheme. Usually the following categories of change will suffice:

- *major* – big changes, perhaps managed as a project;
- *normal* – individual changes; most will be of this type;
- *emergency* – needed as a result of an incident.

A word on emergency changes: it often happens that IT staff at first fail to plan ahead and log their changes in plenty of time for them to be assessed at a CAB. This doesn't mean the change is an emergency and you shouldn't allow it to be logged as such. The emergency change category should be reserved for those changes that have suddenly become necessary and could not have been predicted, probably as a result of an incident. The process for such changes is effectively the same as that for other types of change, but is executed more rapidly. Be careful not to throw all assessment and control out of the window in the heat of the moment as it may come back to haunt you later.

Authorize (or reject) the change

At the end of the assessment step you will need to make a decision on whether the change can go ahead or not. Sometimes more information is required and the change will remain in the assessment step until that is provided. The change may also be rejected outright if it is judged not to be required or justified. But assuming it passes the test, the change will then be flagged as 'authorised' and the relevant person (who may or may not be the submitter) can go ahead and implement it. The date and the person authorizing the change should be recorded. Ideally this should be someone different from the assessor, but in a small team this is not always possible.

Implement the change

The change should be approved for implementation at an agreed date and time and there may be conditions imposed that additional testing is carried out first. But, subject to these factors, the change should then be made as planned and the result recorded on the change management record as 'implemented successfully' or 'failed'. If the change was not successful it may need to be removed according to the backout plan that was defined as part of the change request and this should be recorded

5 Implementing IT service management

against the change record. Sometimes backing out the change is not the best approach and a further change request may be raised to correct the unwanted effects of the first one.

Case in point

> A project was in the middle of implementation, with some modules live and others in test. The project team deal directly with the supplier of the application to report bugs in both environments. The supplier would dial on to the server and make whatever amendments it thought was necessary. The trouble was the customer never knew when the changes were being made or what else they would affect. Live users complained bitterly that, whilst some bugs were fixed, they never knew from day to day which functions would work and which would be suddenly and mysteriously broken.

It may be useful to maintain a forward looking picture of which changes are scheduled for implementation and when, in order to identify potential conflicts and inform the relevant parties of when systems may not be available for use. This is often called the 'change schedule'.

Review the change

As well as assessing change requests, the CAB will also review changes that have been implemented after around one or two weeks to check that there have been no unexpected implications from it – for example, increased numbers of incidents reported to the service desk.

Close the change

Once reviewed, the change request can be closed.

These are the major steps involved in a change management process. Each step will have a status associated with it between which the change request moves. These are usually similar to the following:

- logged;
- being assessed;
- authorized;
- rejected;
- implemented;
- failed;
- closed.

Control processes

As with most of the IT service management processes you will want to keep an eye on the emerging trends in the number of changes submitted and their success in implementation. This will allow you to identify any improvements that could be made to the effectiveness of the process and provide you in the long term with better results.

Summary

- Change management is all about managing the risk of change to your (hopefully) stable live environment.
- Each change request should be logged, assessed, approved, implemented and reviewed as part of the process.
- Details like backout plans and proper testing are essential and should not be missed out.
- Emergency changes are fast-tracked through the process, but only if they are genuine emergencies in response to an urgent need to restore service to users.

Next steps

1. Check to what extent your existing service desk system supports the process of change management; if it doesn't, you will need to decide whether to replace it or work around the limitations with spreadsheets, etc.
2. Define your change management policy and process with input from your team.
3. Identify the changes you will treat as service requests.
4. Start to log changes and hold CAB meetings to review them.

Release and deployment management

Objective

To deliver, distribute and track one or more changes in a release into the live environment.

It is relatively unusual nowadays for a small IT team to develop its own bespoke software and hence the classical process of release management takes on less importance than it does in a traditional software

5 Implementing IT service management

development environment. However, the process as a whole is still relevant to ensuring that the packaged applications used within the organization are rolled out in a controlled way.

The key points are to:

- define what your policy is with regard to release management – for example, how often you will upgrade key applications and how long you will wait after new versions have been made available;
- ensure that new releases of software go through the change management process so that they are planned and assessed appropriately;
- have an acceptance test environment to allow users to check that the new release works correctly before putting it live;
- maintain a full picture of what applications are installed, together with their versions and end of support dates;
- create a plan to control the release of new versions at the appropriate time – for example, when the next version of your office application will be distributed to all users and whether it will be piloted first.

Case in point

> We have previously done some work for a major library that packaged its software changes for a specific application into twice-yearly releases that they called the 'Halloween' and 'Beltane' releases.

Effective planning of new releases via change management will ensure that incidents and problems are minimized and service to users is disrupted as little as possible.

If you are in the game of developing your own software, then release management may take on more importance for you. You will need to decide how often you will package multiple changes into a release for implementation. The release frequency will depend upon an agreement with customers as to how long they can wait for changes to be developed and put live, and will go hand in hand with the classification scheme of 'major', 'normal' and 'emergency' that we mentioned earlier. As well as regular scheduled releases you may need to define a process for delta releases containing those changes that the business simply can't wait for. The key point here is to agree it with the customers and integrate it into your change management process.

Control processes

Summary

- Release management is about grouping related changes together for implementation at the same time.
- For packaged applications, much of this will have been done by the supplier before you receive the software.
- For bespoke development, you will need to define a release policy for each application which sets out the type and frequency of releases.
- Release management needs to be implemented in close co-operation with the change management process.

Next steps

1. Create a catalogue of your installed software and its version(s).
2. Review whether you need to group software changes into releases and how this will work with your change management process.

Configuration management

Objective

To define and control the components of the service and infrastructure and maintain accurate configuration information.

Configuration management (or, to give it its full ITIL name, service asset and configuration management) is an area that can be as wide as you want to make it. Basically it is about knowing what you've got, where it is and ideally how the various parts of your IT landscape relate to each other. Traditionally this has meant hardware assets, but increasingly organizations are recording and tracking a variety of other types of asset, such as services, software, documentation, and even people.

The benefits of effective configuration management can go far beyond the ability to produce a listing of all your IT equipment for insurance or financial auditing purposes. The configuration management database (CMDB) acts as a supporting repository of information that is useful in other IT service management processes such as incident, problem and change management. The end goal is to create a comprehensive map of

5 Implementing IT service management

how your IT services are delivered, including the relationships between business processes, IT services, applications, servers and networks, so that the impact of losing one of them can be fully assessed.

There are a number of different ways of approaching this area: some organizations adopt a top-down method starting from their service catalogue and then mapping out the components of each service at various levels such as application, network and server. Others start from the bottom with hardware and work upwards towards the services. Both approaches are valid; for the purposes of explaining the principles we'll take the second of these and begin with the hardware assets.

The process of getting your hardware under control consists of five steps, and we will consider them in order.

The steps are shown in Figure 8.

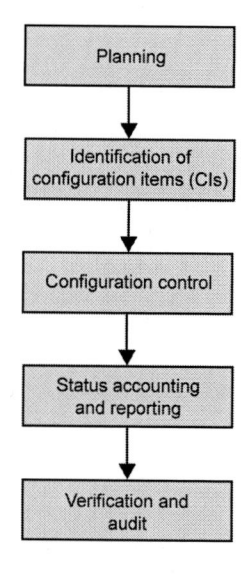

Figure 8 – Configuration management steps

Planning

Before starting to record and control your assets you'll need to decide some basic planning parameters, such as:

- *How will the exercise be resourced* – both in the implementation stages and the ongoing operation of the process? If you currently have no records at all then it may be a big job to start collecting data about configuration items, especially if you decide to cover a

wide range and don't have a software tool to help. Can you get any other business departments to help for example, if they keep an inventory? Should you bring in external resources at key stages?
- *What is the scope of the items you're going to bring under control* – for example, all locations, all departments, all domains? This will make a big difference to the scale of the task facing you. Sometimes it's better to phase this in, particularly if there are discrete dividing lines you can use (e.g. office locations).
- *What are the specific benefits you're planning to deliver and how can they be measured?* – As always, try to be clear about why you are doing this from the outset – how will the captured data be used?
- *How long will it take?* – Obviously this will depend upon the resources available, which, in turn, is a function of the budget you have. Are there any other dependencies such as year-end that make it desirable to be ready for a particular date?
- *What tools will you need to use?* – Will you need to buy any (see Chapter 8 for guidance)? A carefully selected software tool can save you a lot of time over the next few months and years, but it won't do it all for you.

These and other relevant questions should be answered in a Configuration Management Plan that defines where you're going before you set out, and how you will know when you've got there.

Identification

Having done some basic planning you next need to make some decisions at a more detailed level.

First, which types of device are you going to record and track? In order to work out what you will or won't record you will need to set out some decision criteria, such as:

- *cost* – is there a minimum value below which the effort of recording a device outweighs the benefit? For example, most organizations don't track keyboards and mice, preferring to regard them as 'consumables'. Of course, this is a movable feast as the cost of hardware generally falls over time so keep an eye on the next few years when making this decision;
- *security* – devices that hold data and are vulnerable to theft (e.g. laptops and PDAs) probably require more attention. More laptops are stolen than desktops so you are more likely to need the details of these for insurance or crime reporting purposes than larger, more secure devices;
- *legal* – you may be bound by regulatory authorities to track certain items – for example, for PCI DSS compliance (Payment Card Industry Data Security Standard) in retail.

5 Implementing IT service management

There are usually some items that cause debate – such as monitors – especially as the cost of hardware continues to fall. A deciding factor is often whether you have an automated tool that can discover these devices and so reduce the effort required to track them. At the end of the day, it's up to you, there is no hard and fast rule. Draw the line between cost and benefit where you believe it should be and move on.

Secondly, what attributes of the devices you have selected do you want to record? If you record too many then you will be creating an administrative burden; too few, and you could find that the data is less useful than you had hoped. Obviously you need to be able to distinguish between one item and another, so serial number and machine name (e.g. for PCs and laptops) are a must. If your hardware is asset-tagged, you will almost certainly want that information too. Beyond these basics we then get into two main groups of attributes: technical and non-technical.

The technical attributes are going to be those such as memory, disk configuration, manufacturer and model, and these areas are best addressed by an automated tool if you have one (if you haven't we recommend looking at getting one).

We then have the non-technical attributes – such as cost, supplier, purchase date and purchase order number – which no tool currently on the market is going to automatically provide for you. You need to think carefully about which data you really need to record against each item and how you're going to obtain it and update the CMDB in a timely fashion. For financial information you're either facing a lengthy trawl through past purchase orders and invoices or you will make a decision to start recording it for new items only from a set date, for example the start of the financial year.

Often the most difficult attribute to capture is one of the most useful – location. In order to provide meaningful reports and audit your CMDB, you will usually need to know where items are supposed to be so that you can physically go and see if they are genuinely there. The ideal would be to have a method of automatically capturing location or deriving it from some other attribute – for example, network address or network directory – but this isn't always possible. If it is not possible then you will need to ensure that any IT staff who regularly move kit know to update the CMDB when they do it and make it clear to users that they should not move things themselves without letting IT know.

Of course, the data you need may already exist in other places within your organization, such as finance or HR systems. If you can access this information in an effective way then this could form a logical part of your CMDB – usually known as a 'federated' approach. The data stays where it currently is but is brought together by some means, such as a query tool, to produce a useful composite view or report.

Control processes

Control

Having decided what you're going to track and the attributes you want to capture, the next step is to start collecting the data. If you are very small or on a single site this could be done manually, but in most cases a discovery tool will help and there are plenty available that will do the job without costing too much. Such a tool will scan your network, find devices and then gather information about them using a variety of methods. It should then ideally interface into your IT service management system to create configuration items that can then be linked to incidents, problems, changes, etc. as required.

But such a tool may not be able to detect all of the items that you wish to record so you will probably end up carrying out a part manual, part automatic data collection exercise. Devices that don't have the on-board intelligence to provide information about themselves via SNMP (Simple Network Management Protocol) or client installation (such as some barcode scanners or monitors) may need to be visited and reviewed for serial number and related information. Be aware also that devices that are turned off or simply not on the network when a discovery scan is performed won't respond and so won't appear in your inventory yet.

If you have decided to record information about location of servers in a rack then this too will require a certain amount of legwork.

Status accounting and reporting

As part of keeping your CMDB up to date you will also need to implement some form of process to handle the life cycle of a device, from the addition of new ones, the tracking of changes to them and finally their disposal. Of course, such changes should be going through your change management or request fulfilment process, so you should be aware of them. If you are using a discovery tool then you may have the option of creating a new device manually in your IT service management system with a minimum of details (such as the serial number) and then allowing the tool to 'fill in the blanks' once the device has been installed and discovered.

Throughout their life cycle, configuration items will be in one of a number of 'states', such as:

- installed;
- in stock;
- in repair;
- disposed of.

The trick is always to ensure that each item is in the correct state through a combination of automated and procedural controls. Take the time to

5 Implementing IT service management

define your procedures carefully and ensure that all IT staff are aware of them. Use the discovery tool to identify cases where correct procedures may not have been followed and clamp down on non-conformance in the early stages before your CMDB gets too far out of sync with reality.

For various reasons you will want to produce reports on the information held in your CMDB and you will need to be able to differentiate between equipment that is in use and that which has been scrapped long ago. Some of the reports you may want to produce are:

- installed kit by manufacturer and model – this may be useful to provide to a hardware maintenance supplier to use for quotes or as the basis of a contract;
- number and value of items by location – useful for auditors and insurance companies alike;
- number of PCs with less than a specified amount of installed memory – to assess the impact of upgrading to a later version of an operating system or office package.

Once you have the information at your fingertips it's surprising how useful it can be in a wide variety of circumstances. Review your uses of the data on a regular basis to check that you're not expending valuable time to collect information that is unlikely ever to be used.

Verification

Depending on how good your tools are and how well your procedures update configuration item status, your CMDB will be more or less accurate. But it's wise to confirm or contradict your suspicions on a regular basis (especially in the early days) in order to build up a degree of confidence in your data and identify improvements to your process. That's where the verification audit comes in.

It is usually best to create an audit programme that covers each of your main sites over a period of time, tailored to the available resource and the findings of previous audits. If you have audited a site before and your CMDB records have shown a high degree of accuracy then you could visit that site relatively infrequently, so saving time and money. If, however, your CMDB report of what should be at that site bears little or no relation to what is actually on the ground then further investigation and regular checking will be the order of the day. The likely end result is that the quality of your data should improve over time and accordingly your audits become less frequent.

Control processes

Beyond hardware assets

We started this section by saying that configuration management is more than just hardware asset management. The degree to which you are able to progress beyond this will depend upon your exact requirements, level of commitment, time available and the functionality of your IT service management system. Most systems allow the definition of other types of configuration item – such as software, documentation and service – and you will need to carry out the same process as with hardware to define the attributes you wish to record. Again, a discovery tool can help with the tracking of desktop software to some extent, but for other types you will almost certainly need to enter your data manually. However, if you keep the level of items relatively high this need not be too onerous.

If you undertake any bespoke development it may be useful to create configuration items to represent different modules or databases. Requests and changes can then be linked to these items and reported on later to give an indication of where the areas of significant change are. Similarly, creating configuration items for important documents will allow you to keep track of changes to versions of them.

The question of representing meaningful relationships between configuration items is often the one that sorts the mature ITSM systems from the less mature. Ideally you will be able to create links of different types between items such as:

- an IT service 'uses' an application;
- an application 'runs on' a server;
- a server is 'connected to' a network.

... and perhaps even be able to show them in hierarchical diagram form. In theory, at least, this may be useful during the impact assessment stage of change management as it will show what else will be affected by a change to one component of the infrastructure. If you have the time, linking support documentation to the items they document – for example, servers or systems – will highlight the need to update them if a change is made, so keeping current all aspects of the service. An example could be your IT Service Continuity Plan, which could be linked to the servers and systems that are included in it; if one of these systems is decommissioned, the Plan will need to be updated to reflect the new situation.

In a small IT operation this may be of limited use as the relationships may be well known without needing to document them, although it may be helpful for new IT staff who do not yet know the set-up too well. Experimentation is required to establish what would be relevant and useful to you.

Summary

- Configuration management has the potential to give a small IT team a good degree of control over their assets and allow them to make more informed decisions.
- However, a balance needs to be struck between the information that is collected and the effort involved in maintaining it, and the specific objectives for your organization should be clear before embarking upon the establishment of a CMDB and associated process.
- The use of an automated discovery tool will help significantly with capturing and tracking your hardware assets, but you need to make sure the one you choose can pass at least some of its data into your service desk system.

Next steps

1. Create a plan to roll out configuration management in your organization.
2. Start to define what you will track as a configuration item.
3. Look at what tools will be useful.

Relationship processes

The relationship processes encourage the small IT team to look both ways towards the business and towards its third party suppliers to ensure that adequate communication happens and that the organization receives the level of service it pays for.

Business relationship management

Objective

To establish and maintain a good relationship between the service provider and the customer based on understanding the customer and their business drivers.

How is your IT team's relationship with the business it serves? Chances are it's OK on a day-to-day basis: people are generally friendly and you probably have some banter going on with users who call the service desk.

Relationship processes

The business may involve IT when there's a specific project to be achieved, such as a new system or a large office move. As IT Manager you may have regular meetings with your boss to discuss any issues such as budgets and staffing. Yes, it's OK. But it could be so much better.

The typical problem with this limited degree of interaction between IT and the business is that things tend to stay pretty much the same; the same services are delivered in the same way year after year on the assumption that that's what the users want because that's what the users have always had. This can lead to a sense of detachment between the IT department and the rest of the business. The real issue is that often the business doesn't understand IT; it doesn't see why some things take so long to do or why they cost so much – 'surely you just press a button' is a phrase often heard by many a frustrated IT manager.

Case in point

> The authors have come across a number of extreme cases of this. In one company, the IT team was literally housed in a hut in the car park and this summed up their level of interaction with business management. The IT Manager received the same budget year on year and decided in isolation what to spend it on, effectively guessing what the business priorities might be. Not surprisingly, the reason the authors came across this company was because they were looking to outsource their IT – which they eventually did. IT was seen as a pure cost – a necessary evil to be cast out at the first opportunity.

Imagine the IT department was a small business and the users its customers – if it didn't have a monopoly how long do you think it would last? The key to improving the relationship with the managers and users within the company is to realize that the IT team needs to do many of the things a small business does, such as:

- understand who your customers are;
- understand what your customers want;
- market your services continually;
- deal with customer complaints fairly.

Over the next few pages we will deal with each of these areas and hopefully give you some ideas that can help you to get closer to your business.

5 Implementing IT service management

Understand who your customers are

Let's start by revisiting the difference between a 'customer' and a 'user'. A customer is someone who pays for the service you provide. Typically this will be a business manager who holds a budget from which a charge is made for IT services. The level of detail given for the charge can vary and often IT costs are lumped in with other centralized overheads, such as finance and HR, so it can be difficult for the customer to know exactly how much is being paid for the IT component. This can make it hard for the customer to reach any conclusions as to whether he or she is receiving value for money for the IT services being supplied.

A user is the end recipient of the IT service, usually someone who needs to use an IT system to get the job done. Of course, a customer can also be a user.

So your first step will be to create a list of who pays for your services. Your finance department may be able to help with this as it controls the allocation of budgets. Information such as their contact details and how much they pay (or at least what proportion of the total cost they pay) will also be useful. You may wish to take this list a step further and include 'stakeholders' in the IT service. These are people who do not necessarily pay for or use the IT service directly, but have an interest in, and are affected by, the way services are provided. This may include groups such as the company's customers, its suppliers and perhaps its board of directors.

Understand what your customers want

Now that you know who your customers are, you need to ask them what they really want. The key point in this is that we are talking about the existing services provided, rather than requirements for new systems. The latter is typically often discussed at management meetings and the IT Manager will usually be aware of these areas. But the delivery of services that are already in place is all too often overlooked, especially if the services have been running for some time.

The best way of doing this is really up to you; it may be appropriate to have a single meeting with all customers in attendance or you may decide to go and see each person individually. This may partly depend upon the general appetite to discuss IT issues; often business managers are initially reluctant to dedicate time to IT as it is not seen as being central to their role. It is the authors' experience, however, that once this initial resistance is overcome, both parties come to regard such discussions as valuable. If you are assured of a reasonable attendance, a single meeting could work well. Otherwise there is no substitute for a good old-fashioned one-to-one meeting. A combination of the two might suit some people; or does the customer have a regular

Relationship processes

departmental meeting that you could take a slot at on a regular basis? The format doesn't matter that much – the important thing is that everyone gets a chance to express an opinion about the current IT service.

Case in point

> IT saw this particular office as always complaining and the office staff thought the IT service was terrible. Eventually the IT Manager arranged the first of a series of business relationship meetings to discuss the issues. Once they were face to face, IT started to appreciate the pressure that the staff were under, and the Office Manager admitted that most of the complaint-generating issues had not even been logged with the service desk. After three or four constructive meetings, the office became a champion of the IT service and encouraged other departments to have similar meetings.

These meetings go hand in hand with some of the areas covered within the service level management process. It helps if you have a service catalogue setting out the services you currently provide as a basis for the discussion. Some reports setting out that customer department's use of the services would also be useful, for example:

- the number of incidents logged at the service desk;
- average turnaround times of requests;
- types of request made;
- the availability of the main systems they use.

The key questions to discuss at the first meeting with the customer are as follows.

- What are their general impressions of the current IT service?
- Are we providing the right IT services?
- Are we providing them in the right way?
- Do they regard the current IT service as good value for money?
- What other services might be useful?
- What issues do they currently have that have not been resolved to their satisfaction?

Be prepared for the first few meetings to seem a little negative. This is the first opportunity for the customer to raise possibly several years' worth of issues and it is important that you avoid becoming too defensive. You may find that some of the issues raised are easily fixed; in

5 Implementing IT service management

fact, it's not uncommon to find that they haven't been reported to the service desk at all. However, as subsequent meetings progress, you should find that the mood lifts as a better mutual understanding develops.

The frequency of meetings should be adjusted over time according to the number of issues to be discussed. Often they will start off as monthly and then reduce to quarterly or six-monthly over the first year. Where the relationship has stabilized sufficiently, an annual review meeting will suffice as long as this is agreed by both parties. An important consideration is to make sure that all meetings are minuted and actions recorded. This will avoid any disputes later and act as valuable evidence when you are subject to an internal or external audit.

Market your services continually

It is probably fair to say that most of the unreasonable requests that come from users into the IT department are based upon a lack of understanding rather than a desire to annoy. This is why it's important for the IT team to do everything it can to make sure that users know what services are available, to what timescales and what's involved in delivering them.

This needn't cost the earth, as a variety of methods are usually in place within the company that can be used to communicate to users. These may include:

- an internal magazine;
- team/core briefings;
- the intranet;
- email.

Traditionally IT has not used these channels to communicate proactively in the same way as other parts of the business, such as HR, relying instead on an occasional brief email when a service is not working. Obviously this gives rise to the perception that 'IT only communicates when it's bad news'. Use whatever methods are available to you to let users know about items such as:

- news – for example, new services or improvements to existing ones;
- hints and tips;
- dos and don'ts – for example, for information security;
- service level targets;
- results of user satisfaction surveys;
- upcoming major changes.

As well as these standard communication methods there are a number of other ways in which the IT team can make itself and its work better known, for example:

Relationship processes

- educational events such as IT roadshows or open days;
- host a regular back-to-the-floor day for managers of other departments to spend a day in IT;
- participate in internal cross-communication initiatives, such as 'My job in 60 seconds';
- publish leaflets setting out key IT-related information, such as the SLA or information security policy;
- send out a regular IT newsletter via email;
- get articles published in industry magazines.

Don't expect fast results necessarily but over time you will find that these activities make a huge difference to the way in which the IT department is perceived within your company. It can be a long road, but keep plugging away and you and your users should find it worthwhile.

Deal with customer complaints fairly

Things don't always go to plan and sometimes customer service is not what it should be. In the same way as a consumer would expect to be fairly treated by a retail organization so the IT department should try to ensure that customer and user complaints are thoroughly investigated and resolved. The idea of encouraging users to complain seems counter-intuitive but the principle behind it is to get them to tell you about issues rather than to ignore you and tell everyone else. Surveys in the past have concluded that unhappy customers who don't complain tell an average of seven other people about their bad experience. In a small organization it will not take long for such issues to become common knowledge, therefore undoing all the hard work you've done in promoting your department within the company. You also will not get an opportunity to fix what was perceived to be wrong or to achieve the satisfaction that comes from turning a complainant round to be a supporter through prompt and effective treatment of the complaint.

The first action in this is to ensure that an adequate complaints process is in place and agreed with the customers of the service. This is something that can be discussed at your regular customer meetings. Once in place, it should be published appropriately – for example, in the SLA and on the intranet – and staff trained in how to follow it. If a complaint is made it should be investigated, acted upon, reported and formally closed according to the process. As part of your continuous improvement activity you should track the number of complaints received, but remember the number is likely to go up at first as you will be encouraging users to log complaints. Hopefully the number should peak before you can then start to try to bring it down to an acceptable level.

5 Implementing IT service management

Summary

- A small IT department has a lot in common with a small business: it needs to know who its customers are, what they want and to market its services continually through a variety of methods.
- Business relationship management can be one of the most rewarding aspects of IT service management for both the business and the IT department.
- The key aspects are to identify the customers of the service, talk to them openly about the services provided and act on their feedback, whether it's good or bad.
- Creating a plan to inform as many people as possible within the business about your services will also bear fruit over time, but expect this to be a long and ongoing process.

Supplier management

Objective

To manage suppliers to ensure the provision of seamless quality services.

External suppliers are a key component in the delivery of an effective IT service. There is no way a small IT team can do it all so having a commercial relationship with a third party that has either the skills or the resources (or both) that your team lacks is a must. But it's surprising how often such relationships are based on the vaguest of foundations; an unclear definition of what is to be provided with few checks that the correct service is being received. Sometimes the only part that flows smoothly seems to be the payment. Such situations can be avoided by taking a few straightforward steps to getting your supplier management on a firm footing.

Supplier strategy

The first step is to review your supplier strategy if you have one or to create it if you don't. This may fit within your existing IT strategy where it covers the sourcing of goods and services to meet your needs. It needn't be a long-winded document as long as it covers the areas in which you provide services and your preferred approach to delivering them, whether via in-house skills or via the engagement of outside help.

Relationship processes

As part of this it may be useful to categorize your suppliers on a matrix of spend vs. risk as follows:

- high spend, high risk–strategic
- medium spend, medium risk–tactical
- low spend, low risk–commodity

It's up to you which of the above categories you allocate to the intermediate points on this grid – for example, low spend, high risk – as long as it seems useful to you; there are no hard and fast rules. This helps in a number of related IT service management areas including IT service continuity – what will you do if one of your strategic suppliers ceases trading for some reason?

The supplier catalogue

The next step is to create a supplier catalogue listing all your suppliers and their relevant attributes. As well as the obvious contact details these attributes should include:

- contract start and end dates and notice period;
- value of the contract;
- services provided;
- service levels that are agreed in the contract;
- location of the contract document(s);
- review meeting frequency.

This could be in a document, a spreadsheet or, if it supports it, your service desk system. This helps in being able to see clearly who you are contracted with, how much you are paying and what you should be getting for your money. When tough budget allocations come round in a difficult economic climate you will need to be sure of where you could save money and what the implications to service would be.

Case in point

> The authors are aware of at least one case where an annual support contract included a number of consultancy days to be provided every year, but the customer wasn't aware of this and the supplier didn't go out of its way to mention it unless it was asked. As a result, the customer paid extra every year for a service it didn't receive.

5 Implementing IT service management

Meeting your suppliers

The supplier catalogue will help you to clarify which suppliers warrant more of your attention in the form of meetings and reviews. Of course, there is no need to meet with every supplier in the catalogue; those with whom you only spend a little money and from whom you buy goods or services that are freely available elsewhere are probably only worth a phone call once a year. However, at the other end of the spectrum you may have suppliers with whom you spend a considerable amount and rely upon to deliver your services to users. These are the ones you need to concentrate on to ensure you are maximizing value for money.

Establish a policy of how often you will meet with suppliers according to the category they fall into, for example:

- strategic = quarterly meetings;
- tactical = annual meetings;
- commodity =annual phone call.

Usually suppliers will regard such meetings as useful sales opportunities to introduce you to new products or services and this is fair enough as long as it doesn't become the sole purpose of the meeting. Of course, it's good practice to have an agenda for each meeting and ensure minutes are taken, including attendees, decision points and actions.

Measuring supplier performance

You may have some suppliers who provide a defined level of service, whether it's partial outsourcing or simply help desk support for a key application. You need to have a way of measuring whether you are getting the service you should; if the supplier produces a regular report then that's great, but even then it is desirable to be in a position to check that the information it is giving you is accurate. It's not unknown for a supplier's service desk to downgrade incidents automatically as soon as they approach their resolution target, especially if service penalties are payable.

The main way to do this is via reports from your service desk system and you may need to put some thought into how to tweak your incident management process to be able to tell when an incident was logged with the supplier and how long it took to resolve it. The same principle applies to other types of service whether they be desk-side support, remote monitoring or network provision, and you may need to look at additional tools to help you with this. Most organizations adopt a pragmatic approach: if you are confident that a supplier is providing good service and reports that roughly correspond to your perception of the service delivered then you may decide to accept the supplier's word and not seek to measure the performance yourself. If, on the other hand,

Relationship processes

the reports say the service is good but recent events, such as major outages, tend to contradict that then you will want to spend more time forming your own statistical picture.

When the relationship is over

Sometimes suppliers don't perform. Sometimes customer needs change. Whatever the reason, you need to be prepared for a supplier relationship to come to an end, either as a controlled closed own of a retired service or as a possibly acrimonious dispute. As part of your supplier management process you need to perform a risk assessment on each of your suppliers: how likely is the relationship to end and what would be the impact on your services if it did? For those suppliers you identify as medium or high risk, think about what you can put in place now to lessen the impact (as the likelihood may well be outside of your control if, for example, a company fails). For software products escrow agreements are often put in place for this purpose, but there are other things you can do to make sure you are not left high and dry. For outsourcing relationships ensure that you have a copy of all procedural documentation relating to your systems and try to hold accounts with other third parties, such as network or telephone providers in your company's name, rather than that of the lead supplier. This limits the supplier's power to hold you to ransom in the event of a serious dispute.

Effective supplier management can add significantly to your ability to provide reliable services to your users and give you, as an IT manager, additional peace of mind. Be sure to take the precautions outlined in this chapter and hopefully your supplier relationships will be long and mutually fruitful.

Summary

- A supplier strategy looks at the list of suppliers, the services they provide and their value to the IT team and the business. A risk assessment is a key part of the strategy.
- The supplier catalogue adds more detail about contacts, levels of service, contract start and end dates, notice periods, location of contract documentation, etc.
- Meeting frequency should be based on the importance of the supplier to the organization.
- Even if a supplier provides regular reports, you need to be in a position to challenge its figures with your own.

5   Implementing IT service management

> • Pre-empt problems by having a clear idea of how contracts would be ended if necessary at the least risk to your organization.

Next steps

> 1. List and categorize your suppliers as 'strategic', 'tactical' or 'commodity' – based on the cost and value/risk of the goods and services they provide.
> 2. Decide how often you will meet with suppliers in each category – for example, quarterly for strategic suppliers.
> 3. Create a supplier catalogue covering all of your current contracts; dig out the contract documentation.
> 4. Check whether you are getting the level of service you are paying for from each and every supplier.

Service delivery processes

Here we describe a raft of processes that together fill in many of the remaining aspects of good practice, including service level management and reporting, capacity management, service continuity and availability, IT finance and information security.

Service level management and reporting

Objective

To define, agree, record and manage levels of service. To produce agreed, timely, reliable, accurate reports for informed decision making and effective communication.

Service level management is an important process because it sets the standard by which you will ask to be judged by the business. Drafting and discussing a Service Level Agreement with your customers is potentially fraught with dangers and you will need to be sure of your current service levels before putting any kinds of targets on the table even if they are only supposed to be a starting point. Once expectations are set, they will only move so far.

Service delivery processes

But before we get to service levels, we need to talk about the services themselves as this is often an area that is ill-defined in many IT teams and the organizations they serve.

The service catalogue

Do you know what IT services your team delivers? Many IT managers would say confidently that they do, but when asked to write them down, often struggle to come up with a clear definition at first. This is because there are several different ways of looking at the question. Do we define services from the point of view of the IT department or the business? Do we include those things that we do that the business never sees and so is blissfully unaware of, such as capacity planning or problem management? Is an application a service? How far should we break it down – is provisioning a new user a single service, or is it made up of multiple services such as PC installation, phone installation, user administration and possibly cabling? Some thought needs to be put into what we decide to define as a service as the SLA will be based on our decision.

This is one of those areas where getting both points of view is essential. We would recommend holding a meeting with your IT staff to come up with ideas for a list of services that you believe you currently provide to the business and then comparing this with a similar list produced via a meeting with at least one (ideally more) of your customers. You may be surprised at the results – sometimes customers see activities that you do informally as a defined service whilst remaining completely unaware of what you offer in other, more formal areas. Create as full a list as you can, then consider the number of services you have identified; if the list is too long then it will be difficult to manage and you will be creating administrative problems for yourself; too short, and you may be lacking in flexibility when you come to define target timescales for each of the services. Unfortunately there is no right answer we can give you; suffice to say that you, your team and your customers will know when the list feels about right. Once you have it, it's time to put the list into a service catalogue.

A service catalogue is, in its simplest form, a list of the services agreed as live with details of the description, service type, linkages to supporting services, the business units who use the service (and details of the nominated business owner), the internal service owner, reference to the SLA agreed for this service and various other pieces of information which permit the overall management of the entire suite of live services.

Many organizations actually have several views of the service catalogue:

- a business-focused one which includes everything that a user or customer would easily recognise as being a service they could request and make use of;

5 Implementing IT service management

- an IT-focused one which also includes all the supporting information that is invisible to the user but useful to IT – for example, the applications and infrastructure a service uses.

The information held within the service catalogue is up to you; we'd advise you start with a simple one and expand its coverage over time as the principles become more established within your organization. The service catalogue is a business-facing document of which all of your customers and ideally your users should be aware. Some organizations take it a step further and publish the catalogue on their intranet, turning it into a method by which services can be ordered in the same way as you would from an internet shop – for example, a new PC, a new laptop. If this makes sense for your organization and list of services then by all means give it a go, as long as you are clear about what you are trying to achieve beforehand and can handle the issues of authorization of requests possibly via some kind of workflow.

The SLA framework

A Service Level Agreement (SLA) is, as you might guess, an agreement between the service provider (the IT department) and the service consumer (the customer) to deliver a predetermined level of service in return for certain conditions. Whilst service level management doesn't get into the negotiation of the charges, there is tacit understanding that the SLA is the agreement upon which the charging is based – 'We will charge you as per the arrangements provided that we deliver to you as per the SLA'. Such charging may not be direct in that it may be via the allocation of budget, but the principle still applies.

Service level management is also responsible for ensuring that the supporting resources are in place and controlled sufficiently well to deliver the service. For internal resources the arrangements are documented in Operational Level Agreements (OLAs) and for third party organizations they are documented in Underpinning Contracts (UCs).

Before looking at the contents of an SLA, it's worth considering how you want to structure the SLA framework. Since it's likely that you have several services and multiple customer groups in a network arrangement, you need to consider whether you will create service-based or customer-based SLAs. There are pros and cons with each: service-based SLAs can be difficult to agree when you have multiple customers for that service, each with conflicting demands; customer-based SLAs are often better but can cause extra work to agree changes to services as the entire SLA must be reviewed each time a single service changes. There is no one-size-fits-all for this: you may find it simplest to start with a single SLA for all services to all customers and see how it works in your organization, then adapt as you go along (continual improvement).

Service delivery processes

SLA negotiation

An oft-cited rule is 'if you can't measure it, you can't manage it' – nothing should be included in an SLA unless you can monitor it and measure it; otherwise you run the risk of failing to deliver against your SLA for no reason other than you were flying blind.

We have set out below some typical SLA headings with an indication of what would come within each one – headings in brackets are optional depending on the organization.

1. *Heading* – to start with, there needs to be a heading section that deals with who agreed the SLA, when it was agreed, which services it relates to, when it will next be reviewed and an agreed form of words that lays out what will happen to minor changes during the life of the agreement and under what circumstances the entire agreement may be reviewed.
2. *Scope* – which services are included, which are excluded.
3. *Body* – for each service:
   (a) *Service description* – what it consists of, business functions supported, deliverables, scale, impact to business (you may choose to refer to the service catalogue).
   (b) *Service hours* – the hours during which the service should be available, special exceptions (weekends, bank holidays), procedure for requesting exceptions or extensions, details of pre-agreed maintenance, housekeeping, backup or release slots and procedure for requesting permanent changes to service hours.
   (c) *Service availability* – it's usually best to express this as maximum permissible unavailability, but try not to give technical or meaningless values (99.999% available means little to the business); it's better to say, for example, a maximum of four hours of outage across any one month. Even better if you can relate the specifics of what the outages will mean to the business and can give availability targets around the business processes.
   (d) *Reliability* – the maximum number of outages that will be tolerated over an agreed time frame (e.g. no more than four per annum).
   (e) *Customer support* – details of how to contact support, when it's available, what to do outside the support hours, targets for call answering, incident response and resolution, procedure for requesting support extensions. The incident resolution targets should include and be based upon the definition of incident impact and priority codes and incident classification.
   (f) *Contact points and escalation* – contacts for the customer and the service provider, escalation points and procedure and definition of and procedure for managing complaints and compliments.

5   Implementing IT service management

(g) *Service performance* – details of responsiveness expected of the service (e.g. workstations will respond within two seconds 95 per cent of the time) and the agreed expected traffic volumes, throughput quantities and any known constraints. This should also include details of what system demand will invalidate the targets (for example, if it is agreed that the expected maximum number of concurrent users is 200 for the above target and at the time the target was breached there were 300 users on the service …).

(h) *(Batch turnaround times)* – where relevant, how quickly batches should be processed, what the input and output processes are.

(i) *(Functionality)* – details of the minimal functionality and the maximum number of errors that can be tolerated before the SLA is deemed to be breached.

(j) *Change management* – a brief explanation of and link to the organization's change management procedures to be followed, including targets for approval, handling and implementing change requests for this service.

(k) *Service continuity* – brief explanation of, and link to, the organization's service continuity plans plus an explanation of how the SLA will be dealt with under disaster situations (reduced or amended targets, etc.). There should also be an explanation of the responsibilities of each party during invocation.

(l) *Security* – brief explanation of, and link to, the organization's security policy covering details of any specific responsibilities of each party.

(m) *Roles and responsibilities* – details of the roles of all involved parties and their responsibilities.

(n) *(Charging)* – Details of charging formulae, charging periods, invoicing procedures and payment conditions, and details of financial penalties or bonuses to be levied or paid.

(o) *Service reporting and reviewing* – the content, frequency, timing and distribution of service reports, the frequency of service review meetings and the frequency and procedure for SLA reviews.

(p) *Glossary* – explanation of any terminology used.

(q) *Amendment sheet* – to record any agreed amendments during the period of the agreement.

If the agreed levels of service are fairly common across all services you may decide to list them once and then specify any exceptions; this may make the document shorter and easier to understand. If this is the first time an SLA has been created it may make sense to agree the overall format with the business, including the metrics that will be used, without specifying any actual figures at this stage. This will give you a chance to discuss what types of target would be relevant and meaningful to your customers without getting into the detail of whether a particular number is too high or too low.

Service delivery processes

The next step is to agree some target figures for things like incident resolution timescales and percentage availability. Ideally these will be based upon what the business needs rather than on historical data of what has been delivered, but if business needs exceed that which has previously been delivered then this is where negotiation becomes important. There is no point in putting aspirational targets into an SLA if you know for a fact that, with your current level of resources, they can't be met. You will simply be setting yourself up to fail. The business will either have to allocate additional resources to IT or accept a lower level of service than it says it needs.

If the metrics that the business regards as meaningful are not amongst those you currently collect then the organization may agree to run the SLA in a kind of 'monitoring mode' whereby the actual figures are reported but no targets set for the first few months. This will give the IT team and the business a chance to see what can really be delivered with existing IT resources; again, if this turns out to be lower than the business wants, negotiations will need to be entered into.

Once reasonable targets have been agreed, the intention should be to try to improve performance over a period of time and the targets may be increased year on year. Bear in mind, however, that this should be done in the context of whether it is the best use of resources – if an SLA target is good enough and the business doesn't feel any benefit from better service levels then your IT time and the organization's money may be better spent elsewhere. They will also level off over time once the service can no longer be further improved, so there is a ceiling to improvement.

SLA targets are a useful mechanism for allocating resources or identifying when resources are too stretched. Don't be tempted to implement 'workarounds' to ensure you always meet the SLA if the reason is that you just don't have the resources. Far better to allow the SLA to be breached to show clear evidence that there is an issue. An SLA should not be something the business uses to beat IT round the head with; it serves a useful purpose for IT too in illustrating the balance between resources applied and service levels delivered.

OLAs and UCs

The purpose of Operational Level Agreements (OLAs) and Underpinning Contracts (UCs) is to document how the internal and external supporting teams contribute towards meeting the targets laid out in the SLAs. The key thing here is to fully understand which targets of which services are underpinned by which internal and external team. Often internal teams support most services directly or indirectly whereas external suppliers will supply resources or support for specific services. Once you have identified the relationships between the supporting resources and the services

5   Implementing IT service management

being supported, service level management can work with the relevant team managers to agree what the terms of the OLAs and UCs need to be.

OLAs aren't complicated to write but can take some time to negotiate. The headings of the document will be similar to those for the SLA (see section headed 'SLA negotiation'). Both OLAs and UCs need to be monitored in line with the monitoring of SLA targets and are reported back to team and supplier management contacts in order to ensure continued alignment. Also, any changes to SLAs should be evaluated against the timescales and other terms defined by the OLAs and UCs before the changes are agreed in order to avoid a disconnect between what we promise the customer and what we are in turn promised by our internal and external suppliers. There is no point in promising the business that network issues will be resolved within one hour if your contract with the provider states that they may not even start looking at reported issues for two hours.

Service reporting

In the course of managing your IT services there will be a requirement for a variety of reports, aimed at multiple audiences. These fall into the following two main categories:

1. *Service report* – this covers the information that you provide to people outside IT to show whether you are meeting the agreed service levels, describe what's going on in IT, progress of projects, etc.
2. *Operational report* – information that you need internally within IT in order to effectively manage the services and the resources you have under your control.

If you are fortunate you will have a pre-supplied method of producing the required reports from within your IT service management tool; most tools come with a long list of pre-written reports proudly highlighted by the vendor. Unfortunately it seems fairly rare for these reports to be of significant use without at least partial tailoring to requirements. This means that you will almost certainly end up making use of one of the popular database reporting tools that are on the market to fine-tune or create from scratch the reports you need. Don't underestimate the time this will take or indeed the tremendous value you will gain from having a set of reports that really mean something to you and your customers.

However you produce the reports it is a very good idea to record the method of production. If you create quarterly or even monthly reports, using a number of sources and requiring further manipulation or formatting, you may well have forgotten how you did it last time once report day arrives again; the worst case is that you will end up with

Service delivery processes

inconsistent data because of slight variations in processing and this can be both frustrating and embarrassing.

Of course, every organization is different and the information required will vary widely, but there is probably an absolute core set of reports that will be useful in most cases. We have set out our top four in each category below.

Service reports

- percentage of incidents and service requests closed within SLA target, overall and by customer department;
- number of incidents and service requests logged by month by department;
- number of major incidents by month;
- percentage availability of business critical services.

Operational reports

- incidents and service requests opened and closed by member of staff;
- total number of incidents logged and closed by month;
- total number of service requests logged and fulfilled by month;
- number of incidents open at month end, trend by month (this is your backlog).

Of course, there are many, many more that would be useful but we would advise caution in creating too many; always focus on what action you will take based on the report. If you (or your customer) will never take any action regardless of whether the numbers are large or small or the trend is up or down then ask yourself if you really need that report.

We have suggested above that the frequency of such reports could be monthly, but this is not a given. Again the issue is usefulness and quarterly reporting may well suffice in many cases, particularly for service reports where the customer's appetite will probably be limited. The format of reporting should also be considered; there is a trend towards making the relevant information available regularly (and automatically) via the use of a dashboard on an intranet if you have one. All you need to do then is point your customers at the relevant part of the intranet and they can see their figures whenever they like. In business relationship meetings this would be easy to bring up on a screen for discussion. Be careful, though, to allow the customer to see the figures for its department specifically as well as overall for the organization, as this will be its main focus.

5 Implementing IT service management

Summary

- An SLA is an agreement between the service provider (the IT department) and the service consumer (the customer) to deliver a predetermined level of service in return for certain conditions.
- An SLA can be service-based or customer-based and part of the process is to decide with your customers which structure would best suit your organization.
- OLAs and UCs are agreements with internal and external (respectively) third parties which should support the SLA and be aligned with its targets.
- A service catalogue is a list of the services agreed as live with details of the description, service type, linkages to supporting services, the business units who use the service (and details of the nominated business owner), the internal service owner, linkage to the SLA agreed for this service and various other pieces of information which permit the overall management of the entire suite of live services.

Next steps

1. Document the full list of agreed, live services (into a service catalogue).
2. Determine the approach to the SLA framework (service-based, customer-based).
3. Agree a template for what your SLA(s) will contain.
4. Start negotiating with your customers.

Service continuity and availability management

Objective

To ensure that agreed service continuity and availability commitments to customers can be met in all circumstances.

Service continuity and availability management are separate, but very closely aligned, processes. Availability management looks at the various aspects of how to design and run services and their supporting technology in ways which strive for the highest levels of availability. It is also concerned with the causes of periods of unavailability (whether

Service delivery processes

planned or unplanned), and how such unavailability can be avoided in the future; hence there is a very strong linkage here with problem management.

Service continuity management takes the issue a stage further and looks at what needs to be in place to recover from any events that do occur to a timescale dictated by business requirements. This last part is important as speedy recovery can be expensive and if it's not needed then the organization's money is potentially being wasted.

Let's look at availability management first.

Availability management

The important thing about availability management from the perspective of a small IT team is that it offers a framework for ensuring that the availability required of IT services by the business is documented and designed in to new and changed services. It also ensures that availability is monitored and reported and, where exceptions occur, they are examined, assessed and hopefully resolved. The principle aim of availability management is to ensure that the current and future required levels of availability are measured and achieved.

Let's take a more detailed look at what the general term 'availability' is actually made up of.

It focuses on four aspects, which are generally remembered by their acronym ARMS:

Table 2 – The definition of ARMS

Availability *The ability of a service, component or CI to perform its agreed function when required.*
This basically means the amount of time the component or service is available for use and performing as expected, as a proportion of the time agreed with the customer. So, for example, let's say a service agreed to be available 24x7 has had two outages in the last six months of 2 hours and 20 hours. The total time it should have been available is 24 hours x 183 days = 4,392 hours. Then take away the 22 hours of outage giving 4,370 hours of actual availability. Expressed as a percentage of the agreed hours, this represents 4,370/4,392 x 100 = 99.5% availability.
Reliability *A measure of how long a service, component or CI can perform its agreed function without interruption.*

5   Implementing IT service management

This is measured with the Mean Time Between Service Incidents (MTBSI) or Mean Time Between Failure (MTBF) metrics. Reliability can be improved by increasing the reliability of the components, hence reducing the frequency with which they fail, or by increasing the resilience of the service, for instance, by introducing component redundancy.
Maintainability *A measure of how quickly and effectively a service, component or CI can be restored to normal working after a failure.*
This is measured with the Mean Time to Restore Service (MTRS) metric, which looks at the total length of time taken to restore normal service operation after an incident and divides it by the total number of such incidents that have occurred over a specified time period. NOTE: ITIL cautions against the use of the Mean Time To Repair (MTTR) metric, which focuses more on the time taken to repair the failed component but doesn't necessarily include the additional time it can sometimes take to actually restore the user to full normal working.
Serviceability *The ability of a third party supplier to meet the terms of their contract.*
Where the supplier is bound, by its contract, to support certain levels of availability, reliability and/or maintainability.

Availability management is not just concerned with the technical aspects of availability and reliability; the maintainability aspect takes account of the structure and processes of the supporting organization – for example, if there are resource bottlenecks in the incident management process or there are breakdowns of communication between technical teams. So, although it is common to refer to 'availability', there are generally other factors to be considered and these are sometimes required by the client to be included within the SLA targets. Tread carefully, and make sure you understand both the terms and their historical values within your infrastructure before committing to any targets.

Activities of availability management

The key activities of availability management can be broken into two groups:

1. Proactive activities
   (a) working with the business to understand and document the vital business functions (VBFs) which a new or changed service will be supporting and determining the availability requirements for it;

Service delivery processes

(b) working with project teams to design availability into new or changed services before they go live according to the targets for availability, reliability and maintainability required by the business;
(c) performing risk assessments, managing these risks and, where appropriate, implementation of cost-justified counter-measures;
(d) establishing measures for and reporting of availability, reliability and maintainability.
2. Reactive activities
    (a) investigating all service and component unavailability and, where appropriate, instigating remedial action to provide additional resilience to prevent or minimize impact to the business;
    (b) monitoring, measuring, analysing, reporting and reviewing service and component availability, reliability and maintainability;
    (c) reviewing IT service and component availability, identifying unacceptable levels and the underlying reasons for it.

In addition, availability management produces:

- an Availability Management Plan, which prioritizes and plans IT availability improvements;
- a Projected Service Outage (PSO) document, which takes input from the change schedule, the release schedule, planned and preventative maintenance schedules, testing schedules and service and business continuity management testing schedules to highlight times when service availability may not meet the SLA.

Availability management also gets involved in the design and development processes as early as possible and contributes to the service design in order to build-in support for desired levels of availability.

Availability management techniques

In common with problem management, availability management comes replete with an arsenal of techniques for diagnosing and predicting availability issues. The key ones are outlined here, but the full descriptions of how the techniques work are beyond the scope of this book and better served by reading the appropriate sections in the ITIL manual.

Some of the main techniques are:

1. *Component Failure Impact Assessment* (CFIA) – a fairly straight-forward technique that lists the services being assessed across the top of a table, the components down the left and then an indication at the intersection of a service and a component of either:
    (a) blank to show that the component does not support the service;
    (b) 'X' to show that failure of the component would render the service unavailable;

(c) 'A' where there is an automatically activated alternative component that would continue to support the service;
(d) 'M' where there is an alternative component but its activation must be manual.

CFIA shows in an easily digestible format where the weak points for each service are and which components are most vulnerable.

2. *Fault Tree Analysis* (FTA) – used to predict or analyse the chain of dependencies that have or may cause a service outage. Components are arranged in a tree format showing which components contribute to which functional aspects of the service being analysed, and at each intersection an examination is made of the events dependent upon those components. In this way the FTA can represent information that can be used for availability calculations or testing out hypothetical design options.

3. *Modelling* – used to assess whether new components within a design will match the stated requirements. Simulation, modelling and load testing tools can be invaluable for large scale investments or changes to critical systems; however, in a small organization a spreadsheet package is usually sufficient for this purpose.

4. *Risk analysis and management techniques* – used to assess the vulnerability to failure, the business impact of those failures and the sufficiency of identified countermeasures.

5. *Extended incident life cycle* – looks at the entire process of how an incident played out and tries to identify areas thath, if improved, would reduce the time it takes to restore service. It looks at all aspects from how are incidents detected, how long it takes for IT to be notified and how long it takes for someone to actually start to investigate the issue. It especially looks at those areas where there is 'stagnant time' or time when one part of IT has handed off to either another part of IT (or perhaps the user for more information) or a supplier, but the other party has not yet responded. By reducing the overall time it takes from beginning to end the user can get back to work sooner and the overall duration of unavailability is reduced.

Implementing availability management

In order to implement availability management:

1. Undertake an assessment, with service continuity and with the business, of the vital business functions (VBFs) – i.e. those that are critical to the running of your organization.
2. Document (possibly using techniques such as Component Failure Impact Assessment or Fault Tree Analysis) the relationship between:
   (a) the VBFs;
   (b) the services that support the VBFs;
   (c) the components that support those services
   in order to assess whether the current or proposed arrangement can fulfil the availability commitments required.

Service delivery processes

3. Agree what measures and metrics will be used to measure the required levels of availability.
4. Document the approach to be taken to analysing incidents; which tools are available to be used – both in a reactive mode and after the incident has been resolved.
5. Establish strong interfaces with other processes such as problem management, capacity management and, of course, IT service continuity management. A good and clearly documented liaison between the activities of each process is vital in the effort to improve availability and drive up quality.

Service continuity

So, then we come to service continuity or, more correctly, IT service continuity management (itSCM).

itSCM is hugely important to ensuring the survival of your business in a disaster situation. Many organizations fail to take it seriously enough as it is one of those things, like an insurance policy, that you might spend a lot on and never have to use. However, in the same way as insurance, you don't want to be the organization that decided to 'risk it' and not bother with putting arrangements in place to ensure continuity and survival. itSCM is more than just disaster recovery (but it is that as well); it also covers risk assessment and management and it doesn't have to be used only in 'smoking hole' situations (those where that's all that's left of your server room).

ITIL V3 gives the goal of itSCM as 'to support the overall Business Continuity Management process by ensuring that the required IT technical and service facilities ... can be resumed within required, and agreed, business timescales'. As you will obviously have noted, this is very close to the aims of incident management and those of availability management and, indeed, the three processes have similar goals: to return the user to normal operation as quickly as possible. The point at which incident management and availability management leave off and where itSCM takes over is defined by the business according to what it considers to be a disaster situation. The impact to the business and its ability to continue to remain viable is the key factor here, not necessarily the nature of the event. For instance, the loss of its network might, for an online retailer, be considered a disaster which might necessitate invocation of a continuity plan, whereas for a manufacturing organization it may represent merely an inconvenience.

The IT Service Continuity Plans need to dovetail with the organization's overall Business Continuity Plan (BCP). The creation of this is outside the scope of this book but it can include plans for emergency response, damage assessment, salvage, vital records, crisis management and public relations, accommodation and services, security, personnel,

5 Implementing IT service management

communications, and finance and administration. The creation of a Business Continuity Plan is the responsibility of the wider management of the organization and should not be seen as something IT will do. There is thankfully an increasing trend for organizations to invest time and effort in creating a BCP but (even in these days of pandemics and potential fuel shortages) there are still many without one. If your organization is one of those that doesn't have a BCP then we recommend you start encouraging it to address this issue as a matter of urgency. An IT Service Continuity Plan should still be created even if a BCP isn't in place, but the management must be made aware that there is a danger that while IT services will be successfully recovered, no one from the business will be available to use them.

The activities of itSCM

The key stages of itSCM are:

1. Initiation;
2. Requirements and strategy;
3. Implementation;
4. Ongoing operation.

and we'll go through each of them in turn.

Stage 1 – Initiation

The very first step that should be performed is to gain senior management buy-in. Then, working with the management team, develop a policy which, as a minimum, sets out the management intention and objectives. Next you should determine the terms of reference, scope and responsibilities for all staff across the organization.

Building on the management buy-in, resources then need to be allocated to the tasks associated with developing, maintaining and testing the continuity plans. ITIL recommends that the setting up of itSCM and its relationship with BCM is best handled as a project with the associated resources and control structures this requires.

Stage 2 – Requirements and strategy

Requirements

The main focus in the 'requirements' part of this phase is around performing business impact analysis and risk analysis. Both of these are large topics in their own right (indeed the OGC defines a complete risk analysis framework called M_o_R®), but we will look at them in sufficient detail to get you going:

Service delivery processes

Business impact assessment

A business impact assessment (BIA) seeks to quantify the impact that a particular loss of service would have to the business (financial, reputation, health and safety, breach of the law, loss of market share, etc.). It should examine:

- how the impact will be affected by when the disruption occurs and by how long the disruption lasts;
- what the business understands and agrees to be the minimum acceptable level of service;
- the level of resources, the types of skills, the facilities and the supporting services needed to continue operating at that minimum acceptable level;
- the maximum time the business can permit before the service must be recovered (both to the minimum level and to full recovery);
- the relative priority the business places on the recovery of each service;
- the compound impact to the business of multiple service failures.

BIAs are complex to undertake and need the full support of the business. It is essential that senior management understand, agree with and support the findings of the BIA, but it is equally important that all levels of staff have had their views represented as there are often huge disparities of opinion regarding how much impact the loss of a service would have.

Risk analysis

As well as understanding the impact to the business of the loss or prolonged unavailability of one or more services, it is necessary to assess what the likely, probable and unlikely threats are. This is where risk analysis comes in. Since the purpose is to determine the likely source of threats to the availability of services, this is a technique shared with availability management.

As already stated, there are a number of risk analysis frameworks available and we would recommend using such a structured methodology if you can. The basic principle of risk analysis is to create a list of all possible risks and then a list of threats which could cause each specified risk to occur. This can be done either by detailed analysis of industry data, external identification (e.g. government details of security threat levels), or just by brainstorming.

These risks are then analysed to determine their likelihood and the severity or impact should they occur, both of which should be defined along an agreed scale to ensure that it allows comparison of dissimilar risks. The correlation is often plotted on a two dimensional grid as shown in Figure 9 which, as well as placing each risk into the appropriate

5 Implementing IT service management

intersection, reflects the organization's risk appetite or aversion; the top right corner represents those risks which are both most likely and the highest impact. According to where the organization chooses to 'draw the line', the intersections can be colour coded to show at what point a risk is deemed acceptable or unacceptable.

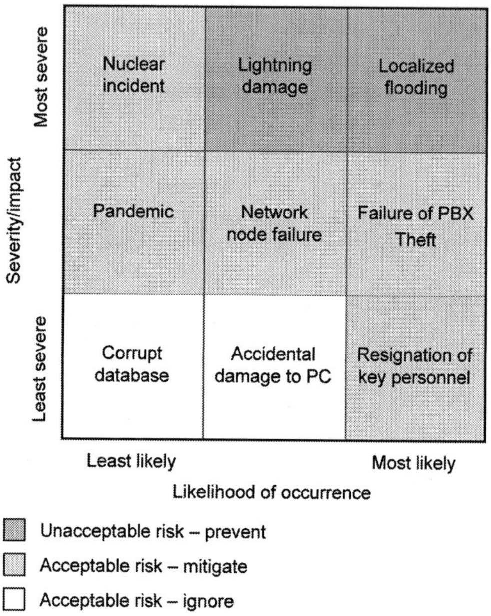

	Least likely		Most likely
Most severe	Nuclear incident	Lightning damage	Localized flooding
	Pandemic	Network node failure	Failure of PBX Theft
Least severe	Corrupt database	Accidental damage to PC	Resignation of key personnel

Severity/impact (vertical axis) — Likelihood of occurrence (horizontal axis)

- ■ Unacceptable risk – prevent
- ▨ Acceptable risk – mitigate
- □ Acceptable risk – ignore

Figure 9 – Risk assessment matrix

Strategy

The second part of the requirements and strategy stage focuses on the creation of an IT service continuity strategy. This takes the outputs from the BIA and risk analysis activities and sets out the approach to IT service continuity based on the identified requirements. It defines the appropriate balance for the organization of measures it will use to reduce or mitigate the identified risks (avoidance, reduction, sharing or retention). Particular attention should be paid to those services identified by the BIA as high impact to the business – these will probably warrant expenditure on measures to prevent occurrence whereas a lower level of impact would more likely suggest one of the available recovery options.

Service delivery processes

Stage 3 – Implementation

Building the plans

Now that you have a strategy that tells you (and everyone else) what services need to be recovered, how quickly and what recovery option has been selected, it's time to put the things in place to enable it to happen in the event you need to invoke the plans.

The IT Service Continuity Plans will give the when, in what order, how, where, and by whom. These should look at much more than just the simple restoration of the systems but also need to consider the service being recovered:

- Are there related systems upon which this service depends?
- How will users access the recovered system?
- How will it be supported if it is being recovered to a remote facility?
- How will the recovered system be backed-up (in case the unthinkable happens and you need to invoke a recovery from the recovery site)?
- And, very importantly, how will you return to normal operations?

Depending on for how long it is anticipated that the service will remain in recovery mode, you will need to consider how change management, incident management and all other IT service management processes need to adapt to take account of the changed situation.

Organization and communications

There needs to be a plan for how IT will structure itself during a disaster; this may not be such an issue for small teams but there will be differences in the levels of authority granted during the crisis in order to permit a quicker response. Consideration also needs to be given to how the resources will interface with the business continuity team and how communications will be managed.

Testing

As each plan is developed, it should be thoroughly tested. Bitter experience has taught us that untested plans either don't work or take far longer than those that have been meticulously tested. There are various methods for testing the plans, each with its own degree of effectiveness and associated costs and disruption:

- *Walk-through tests* are the least disruptive but also the least guaranteed to produce working plans. They should generally only be used to verify that the plans work hypothetically.
- *Scenario tests* are a useful (and fun) way to test the people and management aspects of the plans. They consist of setting a

5   Implementing IT service management

hypothetical scenario and working through how it should be handled. They can be purely table exercises or can include an element of simulated recovery.
- *Partial tests* are good for verifying the recovery of specific servers or elements of a service. It should not be assumed that the aggregate of all the partial plans covering all the components of a service will recover the whole service; there will almost always be a component or an interface that was forgotten or not fully tested.
- *Full tests* are the only real way of verifying that the plan can recover the service. Generally the first test should be performed as soon as possible after the plan has been produced and should be a planned affair that everyone is prepared for. Subsequent tests can be planned or unplanned. You should also bear in mind that there is a possibility that the people who wrote the plan may not be available at the actual recovery (either as they have left the organization or because they were involved in the disaster itself) and so the test should involve people not familiar with the service or the plan to verify that there are no unspoken assumptions.

Stage 4 – Ongoing operation

There are five sets of ongoing activities that need to be performed:

1. Education, awareness and training across the entire organization in general, and the IT department in particular, is necessary to ensure that everyone knows the plan and their role within it.
2. A review of all the plans and schedules needs to happen frequently to ensure that they are still relevant to any changes of circumstances of the organization.
3. Testing should continue to be performed regularly – at least annually, after every major business change and in line with the business needs and the Business Continuity Plans.
4. Change management should assess all changes for their effect on the continuity plans. Change management can also mandate that the plans are updated to reflect the new circumstances that the change will produce and that the plans are tested before the change is implemented.
5. Document control maintains accuracy and consistency of the plans by placing the plans themselves under change and version control.

Invocation

Right, so you have an itSCM strategy and an IT Service Continuity Plan, contracts have been arranged, people have been trained, the plans have been tested, the strategy is reviewed by the management team regularly and still reflects the current organization and then ... the unthinkable happens and a crisis situation occurs. The nature of the situation and the policies you have in place will determine whether your organization

Service delivery processes

deems this to be worthy of invoking your continuity plans. The criteria you have defined will take account of the costs of invoking prematurely.

The instructions on how to invoke, who can make the decision and the immediate next steps should all be contained in your IT Service Continuity Plan, a copy of which should be available in an offline format (in other words, don't put it on the intranet and expect to be able to read it when the network's just gone down) and stored with all key staff both in the office and at home – bear in mind that disasters don't always happen during office hours.

Case in point

> A few years ago one organization suffered a problem with its main production server overnight as a result of an unsuccessful operating system upgrade. The disaster recovery contract was invoked and the system restored to a state of the art facility. Users then found that response times were so much better on the recovery server that the IT Manager negotiated to stay on that server until an upgrade could be bought for the original one.

The invocation decision must be made quickly. This is not always easy as there are situations that can be ambiguous, especially where you are at the mercy of a third party to resolve a situation (for example, a localized power failure might be resolved in minutes, hours or days). The best approach is to set a hard deadline by which resolution must have occurred – if the situation is still unresolved by the deadline then you will invoke.

Recovery options

There are various recovery options that could be employed, depending upon the urgency that the BIA has indicated an outage would pose to the business. Each has its own advantages and disadvantages and each bears a cost and a timescale. It is important to assess each option and negotiate the best deal for the option chosen so as to balance the cost of the recovery option against the cost of the impact of the outage.

1. *Manual workarounds*
   This is often employed as a temporary arrangement while certain services are being fully recovered. For example, phone calls could be manually logged to a spreadsheet, or even paper, until the call-logging system is restored.

5 Implementing IT service management

2. *Reciprocal arrangements*
   Only applicable for a limited number of services but basically it is where two organizations agree to permit access to one of their services in a crisis situation in return for reciprocal permission.
3. *Gradual recovery*
   Sometimes referred to as 'cold standby', this is where accommodation is secured (whether rented or owned) that is fully set up with power, environmental controls, network cabling and telecommunications. In a disaster situation, the hardware and software would possibly have to be acquired or transferred from another location but would be set up and installed. This obviously requires an amount of time and is therefore only suitable for those services which can tolerate a potentially uncertain delay to the recovery time of days or weeks rather than hours or minutes.
4. *Intermediate recovery*
   Sometimes referred to as 'warm standby', this is generally a better option for those services requiring a faster and more defined timescale for recovery than gradual recovery. It enhances the gradual recovery option by utilizing (most commonly) a third party to provide not just the site but also generic hardware, peripherals, communications equipment, and support and operations staff. The facilities are generally offered to multiple organizations simultaneously, in the expectation that not all of them will need the facility at the same time.
   There are a number of disadvantages with this option: physical security can be an issue as the facility has to, by its nature, be flexible to accommodate needs of various sized organizations potentially simultaneously and so securing one area can be an issue. The other issue is that of timescales – even though the site is equipped, it will take an amount of time for staff to configure the site for the requirements of the organization and will then still require recovery time to restore, test and make live the services from the recovery site.
5. *Fast recovery*
   Also known as 'hot standby', this again builds on the previous option. This can be an enhanced agreement with the third party supplier to rent an agreed, fully configured facility with the hardware already pre-configured, tested and ready for action. It then requires only restoration of data, and sometimes even this is catered for by combining the fast recovery facility with an off-site backup storage arrangement.
   Typically the fast recovery option is best for those systems that need to be recovered within a 24-hour window.
6. *Immediate recovery*
   So, this is the top end. The facility can still be either owned or rented but is (a) exclusive, (b) fully pre-configured, (c) fully linked to the 'home' site by communications links which permit some form of data replication or mirroring so that data is fully in sync with the live

Service delivery processes

service, and (d) connected to the client organization's communications network. This means that little or no reconfiguration is required in order for the service to continue uninterrupted in the event of a disaster affecting the home site.

This option is most appropriate for those services requiring no loss of service.

Case in point

> Some organizations are so keen to be sure their immediate recovery option works that they regularly flip across to the backup on a weekly basis. They run on the live and backup servers on a week on/week off basis as business as usual.

Summary

- Availability management looks at the various aspects of how to design and run services and the supporting technology in ways which strive for the highest levels of availability.
- There are four individual aspects of availability, which are generally remembered by their acronym ARMS – availability, reliability, maintainability and serviceability.
- There are a variety of techniques which may be of use in analysing availability issues, including Component Failure Impact Assessment (CFIA), Fault Tree Analysis and Extended Incident Life cycle.
- The major steps in addressing IT service continuity are initiation, requirements and strategy, implementation and ongoing operation.
- IT Service Continuity Plans should be based upon a full understanding of the needs and priorities of the business, assessed and documented via a business impact analysis.
- The recovery facilities you put in place will inevitably be a compromise between risk and cost and may vary from manual workarounds to immediate recovery.

5 Implementing IT service management

Next steps

> 1. Start to gain a better understanding of your IT services and the components that make them up – do you have any single points of failure?
> 2. Begin recording the availability of these items using a monitoring tool and/or major incident records – get an idea of what level of availability you are currently delivering before setting any targets with the business.
> 3. Perform a risk assessment to identify those areas you will need contingency arrangements for.
> 4. Initiate discussions with the business about how long they could cope without each service.

IT finance

Objective

To budget and account for the cost of service provision.

'Now for the interesting chapter', we hear you cry, but wait ... before you fake a yawn and turn to the next one ... please listen up. In order to be able to ensure that there are sufficient funds available to supply the resources and capabilities to deliver the services as agreed with the customer, you need to prepare a budget for IT and the services you deliver. Once the budget has been prepared and agreed and the year is underway, you need a way to track what is being spent, on what and whether it matches the predictions made at the budgeting stage. The third aspect is largely dependent upon whether your organization charges for internal services. If it does then you need some way to determine the appropriate charging mechanism for the services and a way of monitoring this throughout the financial year.

This group of activities has various names – financial management for IT services, budgeting and accounting, service economics – but, for simplicity, we'll call it IT finance. In a small IT team the process is usually managed by the IT Manager, supported by the finance or accounts function of the organization. It should be noted that IT finance does not cover all aspects of accountancy such as taxation or the legislative sides of accounts – these aspects are best left to the experts. In fact, in terms of agreeing IT's budget and monitoring spend against it, this is almost always catered for in great part by existing financial procedures and regulations within the organization, overseen by the Finance Director or equivalent. This normally consists of an annual round of discussion

Service delivery processes

concerning priorities and desired expenditure for next year, followed by a bit of negotiation and finally the setting of the budget (or budgets).

But, beyond the mandatory calculating of budget and accounting for expenditure, there is another layer of cost-related information that can prove very interesting to the IT Manager intent on improving his/her IT service management, such as the costs associated with services and changes, and we'll look at these areas too.

IT funding

There are basically three stances that IT can adopt with regard to how it funds itself:

1. Accounting centre
   This focuses on the correct recording of the costs of providing the services and uses only the budgeting and accounting activities. There are still benefits with this model as the use of a clear and consistent budgeting and accounting system means that better planning and assessment of costs and risks are possible, but it does not give much flexibility to the IT organization to govern itself.
2. Recovery centre
   This requires that, in addition to accounting for the costs, they are apportioned according to the cost model and are charged to the customers. The net aim is to balance the books (no profit, no loss). This has the advantage that customers are directly affected by increases in their demand, provided that the cost model is correct and fair.
3. Profit centre
   It is not uncommon for the IT function to be run as a separate legal entity with business objectives set by the organization but with sufficient autonomy to manage itself. The key point is that a clear price list is established and customers order much as they would from any other third party supplier. Since the objective is to recover an amount greater than the costs incurred, there will need to be visibility of the mark-up being added and the profit margin being made.

We'll have a look at the methods used for each of these approaches.

Budgeting

Budgeting is (in the words of ITIL) 'the process of ensuring that the correct finance is available for the provision of IT services and that, during the budget period, they are not overspent'. That means that it is not just a set of activities that are performed once a year and then forgotten about. It is a continuous process and forms part of the overall control that is exercised over how services are provided.

5 Implementing IT service management

As mentioned at the beginning of this section, the process should be closely bound up with the organization's financial cycle in order to reduce replication of effort and to underpin the accounting and charging aspects of the process. There must also be a close alignment with the overall organization budget as spend on IT services can, in some organizations, be a large part of the organization's total spend (sometimes rivalling or even exceeding the people costs). The process may also be under constraints imposed by the business as a result of organizational change or cost cutting, or the departments that fund IT may have limits on revenue or capital spending to which IT must adhere.

The budget should take account of current operational activities, anticipated changes to operational activities (whether reducing or increasing) and anticipated projects, but should not go beyond the activities known about within IT. It should work with the other IT service management processes to identify how the organization's needs are predicted to change over the coming year (or further if you are preparing a longer term forecast).

The first step you should make when setting up your budgeting process is to identify all of the budget items; these are the actual, individual items like that server in accounting or the people in the department. In order to do this you need to define a set of budget categories. This will help you to ensure that you don't forget anything and will also allow you to compare month-on-month and year-on-year figures for trends and to identify areas for improvement.

The process of identifying the actual costs of all the budget items can then begin. Some of these you will know in advance as they are part of a contract (e.g. server maintenance) or staff costs – you know what the salaries will be, and possibly what the pay increases are due to be. Some costs are less well understood at budgeting time, or are liable to change, which cannot be accurately predicted, such as overtime, consumables, etc. These are often estimated based on an understanding and projection forward of historical costs. In general, good practice doesn't have that much to say in the area of budgeting and this will be largely dictated by your finance department anyway, so let's move on.

Accounting

Once we have established and agreed a budget and had it approved, we may then decide to work out how we will apportion it throughout the organization. Again, this is an area that varies widely; some organizations don't allocate IT costs to other parts of the business, preferring to simply regard it as a centralized pot. But even if you don't need to do any apportionment within the business there are real benefits to be had in creating a cost model and analysing the resulting figures because it will help to show whether you are spending your IT money wisely.

Service delivery processes

The cost model

A cost model is a way of taking the funds that you have been allocated by the business in your budget and assigning them to customers or services, or in any other way that might be useful to you or your organization. As we've said, a cost model is often used to calculate how much each department should contribute to overall IT costs, perhaps based on numbers of PCs or users; it can also be used for other purposes, but we'll describe this main one first.

Developing a cost model is a large subject in its own right but we'll set out the principal steps and hopefully this will be sufficient to give you the general idea so that you can develop it further within your IT team. You can refer to Figure 10 as an illustration.

The initial step is to identify the cost types you are going to use. These can be whatever makes sense to you, but a common list might look something like this:

- hardware – servers, network equipment, storage, PCs, laptops, etc.;
- software – applications, operating systems, databases;
- people – full costs of employment of your IT staff;
- accommodation – office space, server rooms;
- external services – third party support contracts, network links, disaster recovery facilities, insurance;
- transfer – costs of 'buying' services from within your organization, for example, facilities management.

You may also want to go down another level of detail (referred to as 'cost elements') to subcategorize, using the kinds of examples shown above (e.g. software – applications, operating systems, databases).

Once you have decided on your types, the next step is to determine whether each cost is a direct cost, an indirect cost or an unabsorbed overhead.

- Direct costs are those that can be attributed to a single customer (for example, the costs of the payroll system will generally only be applicable to the payroll or finance department).
- Indirect costs are those that cannot be directly attributed (for example, the hardware costs of the server hosting a number of virtual machines) and thus have to be apportioned to the relevant customers
- Unabsorbed overheads are those indirect costs that cannot be apportioned to a subset of customers and must be apportioned across all customers (e.g. the entire cost of the server room).

Direct costs should be fairly straightforward to allocate. For indirect costs, you need to consider the fairest way to apportion the costs to the

5 Implementing IT service management

customers. This might be to base it on number of users, PCs and laptops, disk storage, etc. It's up to you to agree it with your customers but it needs to be:

- fair to both the customer and the IT department – you need to account for all the costs but not penalize a customer unfairly;
- manageable – don't base the apportionment mechanism on something you can't measure.

For unabsorbed overheads, the apportionment is often done as an uplift proportional to the total other costs applied to that customer – for example, if one large customer accounts for 50 per cent of the overall direct and apportioned indirect costs, then it assumed that it also accounts for 50 per cent of the unabsorbed overheads.

You will next need to determine whether each cost is capital or revenue expenditure and make sure that, for capital costs, only the depreciation is accounted for, not the entire capital value. A final factor is whether the cost is fixed or variable – does it increase or decrease with usage (e.g. overtime)? If it is variable you will need to make a few assumptions about usage volume, ideally based upon past records and perhaps a good knowledge of expected changes during the year.

Once you have identified all of the costs and their allocation and categorization, you should be able to build up a model that shows how the total cost of the IT provision relates to each individual customer (a spreadsheet is often the best tool for this). Your first attempts are likely to need a little tweaking to ensure you feel confident in justifying your calculations to your customers, as this may well have a direct effect on their budgets. Figure 10 shows the process of breaking down the different types of cost to arrive at a figure for each user department.

We mentioned that apportioning costs to customers is not the only use for a cost model. An often enlightening exercise is to try to allocate the costs to specific services in order to come up with a total figure for each service for the year. The same principles apply in splitting costs that are spread across services proportionally – for example, the cost of a network link that provides access to several services could be split according to the number of users of each service at that remote site. This information, combined with knowledge of the business criticality and number of users can give a very good indication of the cost-effectiveness of an individual service. This could help to assess whether the service would be better outsourced, provided with lower service levels or in some cases discontinued completely. Sometimes extremes are shown up via this method where a service that has been in place for some time actually costs a fortune to provide but is hardly used.

Note: Configuration management will provide much of the information regarding how components are related together and form the services.

Service delivery processes

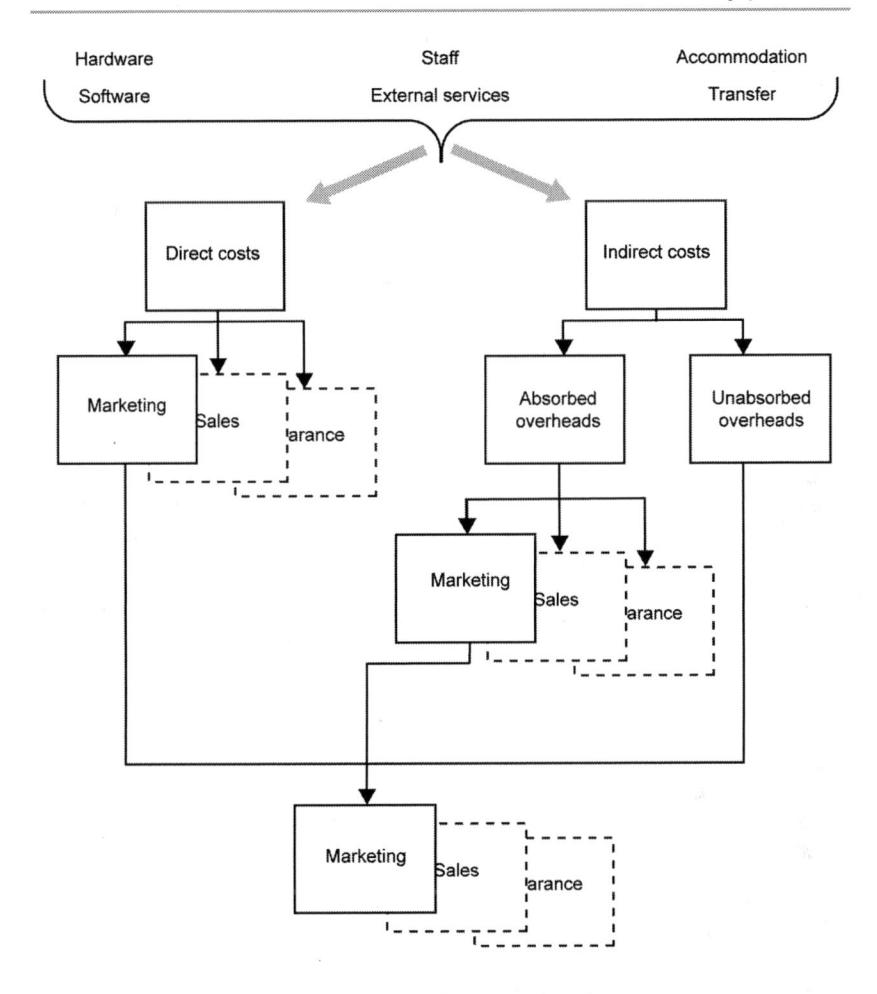

Figure 10 – Cost apportionment by department

This is essential when putting together the cost model as the configuration management database (CMDB) should give valuable information about which services are used by which departments, and any dependencies between services.

Another area where cost models are useful is in change management. Users often request changes of various types with no knowledge of how much it will cost to implement – after all why would they know? Calculating the cost of a change provides IT and the business with a much better idea of whether the requested action is really worth it and helps to discourage users from asking for changes that they themselves would admit (once they knew the cost) they really don't need. Change costing will require that you make some assumptions about the cost of IT

5 Implementing IT service management

labour, perhaps of different types (e.g. developer vs. desktop support) and estimate the number of man-hours needed to implement a change, but this typically isn't hard to do.

A further use of the cost model is the creation of a TCO (total cost of ownership) figure that gives for an individual component, system or service the total lifetime costs associated with it. For example, a server costing £10k with the operating system, installation time, patching and upgrades, maintenance (both contractual and by in-house staff), proportion of overheads (rack space, proportion of air conditioning, electricity), networking connectivity, etc., might actually cost the organization £50,000 over a five-year lifespan. This information can be useful when estimating the cost of the infrastructure parts of new projects.

Charging

And so we come to charging, an aspect of IT finance that is quoted within the good practice guides as an 'optional' activity. This takes the cost model idea a step further by actually setting a price for the use of each service, payable by the customers at regular intervals.

Charging can have several benefits, the main ones being:

- it gives IT a mechanism that enables it to shape customer and user behaviour to ensure we get the best from IT investments;
- it forces the business to control its own user demands;
- it can reduce overall costs by highlighting services with poor cost-effectiveness and low usage;
- it ensures that highly used, popular and important services receive the funding appropriate to their status and need.

In practice, charging can often be seen as overly bureaucratic, unfair or too difficult to manage. These are generally symptoms of a poorly thought-through or implemented charging system, although sometimes even the best and fairest charging systems receive criticism since everyone actually wants their IT to be both excellently provisioned and free. The mantra for charging is that it 'has to be simple, fair and realistic'. It is vital that a charging policy is brought in with the full backing of the senior management in order to ensure that it is seen as mandatory. It is equally vital that the charging policy is designed in full consultation with the department heads in order to ensure that the mechanism devised correctly balances the business view of value for money. This may result in a charging mechanism that at first, does not recover all costs in order to acknowledge the need for certain improvements in quality or consistency of delivery. If a profit-based recovery mechanism is brought in where there are known deficiencies, charging will be resented.

Service delivery processes

The charging model

The most important decisions to be made when setting up a charging model are (a) what to charge for (and what not to charge for) and (b) how much to charge for them (how the charges will be decided/determined).

(a) What to charge for

Generally, it is a good idea to make the chargeable items those that the customer can see as directly delivering benefit to its business functions.

For example, the finance department will see that it uses PCs to connect via the *network* to the accounting system housed in the *data centre*, the corporate email system based on the *Notes server*, the internet through the *firewall* and *proxy servers* and printers through the *print servers*.

Charge them for those items underlined but not those in italics. The customer won't care (shouldn't need to care) about the technical layer below. Work closely with service level management to determine which services the customer believes underpin its business and charge for those.

(b) What to charge for them

Again, this is an area in which IT finance cannot act alone. The charging or pricing policy devised will affect how the service is used: for example, excessive charges levied for network file storage may result in people storing data on USB keys, in email attachments, locally on hard drives or on cloud storage, all of which are undesirable behaviours from the point of view of IT security, IT service continuity, capacity management, incident and problem management, change management ... in short, nobody wins. It is best to set your pricing policies up so that they reward the patterns of behaviour you want to encourage.

You will need to adopt a collaborative approach both with other processes and with the customer to determine what mechanism should be used in order that it is clear, open, fair and simple to administer, and what the resulting pricing model will look like under different scenarios – for instance, what would happen if a new piece of business was taken on that significantly increased payroll activity or internet traffic?

The major ways of pricing are:

- *Cost* – Based either on the total cost of ownership projection for the lifetime of the service or on the costs already actually expended.
- *Cost plus* – Same as cost but with a percentage mark-up (Price = Cost + x%).
- *Going rate* – Price is comparable with other internal departments, either within the same organization or with other similar organizations.

5 Implementing IT service management

- *Market rate* – Price is comparable with third party suppliers.
- *Fixed price* – Agreed price based on negotiations with the customer; usually the fixed price has a finite duration (e.g. price set until December).

You also need to be prepared to amend the agreed policy if circumstances change significantly during the financial cycle. For instance, if you are trying to discourage a high volume of printing, you may have set a high price per page on this but, if a huge and lucrative tender comes in that requires large amounts of printing, be flexible and agree either an exception rate or an amendment to the pricing policy.

IT finance cycles

As mentioned earlier, IT finance fits into the overall organizational finance picture and, as such, needs to adhere to the regular cycles of budgeting, accounting and charging. There are two phases of these cycles: the operational (monthly) cycle and the planning (annual) cycle. Typically budgets will be agreed annually and then monitored monthly with exceptions or changes being managed as they occur.

The cost model will be reviewed and confirmed annually in order to align fully with the budget structure and give a good structure on which to base the charging, and then expenditure will be monitored and recorded monthly through the year. The charging/pricing policy will be established and agreed during the annual planning stage (based on, influencing and influenced by the budgets and cost model) resulting in a published price list, and bills will be compiled and issued to the customers each month.

Within the year it is not uncommon for there to be a quarterly or biannual 'truing up', where budgets are reviewed against actual spend modified by exceptions and changes and, if necessary, an amended forecast is produced that reflects the new understanding of the projected out-turn.

Investment appraisal

So, we've looked at how you might budget, account and charge for existing services, but what about new ones? Investment appraisal is the process used to evaluate whether the business benefit of a new service entirely stacks up.

The two main devices used are:

1. *Return on investment* – how much additional revenue (or lack of loss of revenue) results from the invested amount?
2. *Return on capital employed* – which is a common ratio used by investors to evaluate the overall effectiveness of organizations.

Service delivery processes

Summary

- IT finance consists of budgeting, accounting and (optionally) charging.
- Once you have identified your costs, it is a useful exercise to try to allocate them to specific customers and possibly services.
- There are a number of ways of operating the financial aspects of IT service provision, including acting as an accounting, recovery or profit centre within your organization.
- If you decide to charge for services, ensure your pricing is seen to be open and fair and it encourages the types of user behaviour you regard as desirable.

Next steps

Consider the following questions:
- Do I know the full extent of what I am budgeting for?
- What are the current costs?
- What are the accounting rules and constraints that I need to work within?
- What is the organization's financial planning cycle?
- Should I charge for the services and how should this be done?
- Do I want to break even, make a loss or make a profit?

Capacity management

Objective

To ensure that the service provider has, at all times, sufficient capacity to meet the current and future agreed demands of the customer's business needs.

Imagine driving a car with a broken fuel gauge. You wouldn't know how full the tank was or when to stop for petrol. Worst case, you would run out just at the wrong moment, in the middle of a junction or on a level crossing. In many ways this is the same situation as if you are not monitoring the capacity of your servers and network infrastructure. In capacity terms you're effectively blind and don't know if the next few

5   Implementing IT service management

users or the new application will tip it over the edge into poor performance. Or are your server disks about to fill up, resulting in one or more services to crash completely, possibly at a crucial time such as year end? Will your Finance Director thank you for putting in an unbudgeted emergency request for thousands of pounds for an upgrade to a server halfway through the financial year?

Capacity management is about understanding where you are now with your infrastructure, what is likely to happen over the next six to twelve months and then assessing the impact and planning for it, both technically and financially. It needn't be a difficult area to address and we would recommend the use of appropriate software tools to automate much of the arduous parts of the process. Your aim should be to produce a capacity plan every six to twelve months, aligning it with your budget planning cycle where possible. Of course, not everything can be predicted and the business may come up with the odd surprise during the year that has a capacity implication – for example, a merger or takeover – but even in these circumstances at least you will have the information to hand to understand where you are starting from and which items of infrastructure may need to be upgraded to cope.

Capacity monitoring

The first step is to put in place a monitoring framework that allows you to keep tabs on all of the important components of your services without making an administrative nightmare for yourself in the process. Your configuration management process should be able to provide you with a clear picture of which components support which services, and so what to concentrate on initially. In general it's probably appropriate to start with your mission-critical servers as they would cause you the most pain if they were to stop working.

You could, of course, log on to each server individually on, say, a weekly basis and manually record the key figures in a spreadsheet. If you don't have many servers, that is a reasonable approach to take. If, however, you have too many to make that approach viable then you will need to get some tools to do the work for you. Basic tools are often provided free with the operating system. With a bit of effort in set-up, these will allow you to record the key values from each server and send them to a central point from which you can produce some trending graphs to see in which direction your resource usage is going. If you have some budget available look at what some of the popular network monitoring tools can give you in this area via SNMP (Simple Network Management Protocol) monitoring as they will collect, store and graph all the data you will need with a minimum need for human intervention.

Keeping it simple at first is key; concentrate on your main servers and just look at processor and disk space usage initially. For each server you

Service delivery processes

will need to get to know the profile of usage across the day, the week and the month in order to identify the typical peak dates and times. Once these are known, you can then focus in on these and start to produce trend information for the same peak few hours each week or month.

This initial analysis will give you a good idea about whether your servers are busy, idling or somewhere in between. Often with traditional single-application servers the usage is not too significant, but with the increased use of virtualization this should become more of an involved subject as resources can be shared between applications more easily. Often the vendors of virtualization software will also supply tools to monitor and report on resource usage as part of the deal.

At first, just creating a table listing the servers and whether their disk space and processor usage is high, medium or low will add significantly to your capacity planning knowledge and act as the basis for future planning.

As well as starting to record trend information, many tools allow the setting of thresholds, particularly with disk space used, and will send an alert email or text message if the threshold is exceeded. This is a useful backup to the trend data monitoring as it will identify those instances where the increase in disk space usage is sudden, perhaps because of an application or user error.

But it's not all about servers; there may be other aspects of your infrastructure that play a key part in the delivery of your services, such as:

- network links;
- internet links;
- batch run times;
- backup run times.

These should also be monitored according to the same principles, using tools where available and cost-effective. What you're looking for are trends that, if continued, will sooner or later lead to capacity issues with that resource. Capacity planning is about identifying these early so that you have plenty of time to take some action, such as making better use of existing resources or purchasing more.

Performance tuning

On each type of infrastructure component there are often various parameters that can be tweaked to provide a more appropriate sharing of resources, and this can improve performance. The specifics will, of course, depend upon the component and the manufacturer's recommendations, but it's worth spending some time looking at what

5 Implementing IT service management

could be done to get the most from your existing hardware before opening the cheque book to buy an upgrade. Details of tuning are beyond the scope of this book but, for example, for servers this might involve the correct setting of swap space or repartitioning of disk arrays.

Demand management

Another way to try to avoid the expense of upgrading infrastructure is to go into more detailed analysis of how the existing resources are used, by whom and when. Understanding usage patterns may allow you to identify activities carried out by users (or the IT team for that matter) that are resource hungry but could be done at a time of lower load, i.e. smoothing out the usage pattern. Some negotiation may be required to get users to change working patterns or practices but often they carry out a particular task at a particular time or day without any knowledge of the effects – after all why would they know? Sometimes smoothing out resource usage can mean better service to users as a job that previously took a long time during the day could be run overnight more quickly or at a time of lower daytime usage.

Similarly, with disk space, users tend to be unaware of the impact of loading many large files, such as video clips, onto the server and may be willing to reduce their usage or at least get rid of unwanted files on a regular basis. Software tools that can report on who the biggest culprits are and, if necessary, impose limits on their usage are widely available. You may decide to implement a quota system, but this should be done in discussion with customers and users and set out in the SLA.

Future requirements

Once a clear picture is obtained of the current capacity situation, the next piece in the puzzle is that of the future requirements of the business. The planning horizon may vary but it is usually feasible to know with some degree of certainty what is planned for the next twelve months or so. Of course, the main way to find out this information is to go and talk directly to the business managers who may have the requirements. The corporate plan, if there is one, will also help with this. The discussions should centre on what events might cause extra capacity to be needed in the next twelve months such as:

- organic growth in the number of users of existing services;
- new services or applications;
- mergers and acquisitions that may result in more demand for IT services;
- impending legislative changes;
- use of new technology, such as mobile working.

Service delivery processes

Encourage the business managers to be as specific as possible in terms of numbers, timescales and other factors. Capacity implications should be a regular item on the agenda of your business relationship meetings with customers and you should try to explain why you need to know about significant changes as early as possible. Consideration of the capacity implications of change requests should also be made as part of the change management process.

As well as requirements from the business there may also be an impact on capacity (positive or negative) from some of the plans within the IT team itself, such as:

- introduction of email archiving;
- virtualization of servers;
- keeping server event logs for longer for security purposes;
- reorganization of shared network drives.

These must also be considered and factored into the overall capacity equation.

The Capacity Plan

OK, so we've measured the existing capacity, done some tuning to maximize performance, smoothed out usage where possible and gained a good appreciation of what is likely to happen over the next twelve months or so. It's time to create a Capacity Plan.

This is the document that brings all the pieces of the jigsaw together to generate some recommendations and conclusions. Unfortunately capacity planning is probably still more of an art than science, and although there have been software tools available for many years they tend to remain fairly expensive. The degree of business uncertainty that typically exists, even over a 12-month planning time frame, also makes absolute conclusions difficult.

Having said this, it is certainly possible to reach some cautious indications of what may be required in order to maintain the relevant IT services and to identify those areas in which more time should be spent and on which a more careful eye should be kept.

The Capacity Plan should set out the identified business requirements for the period under consideration, together with their timescales and some indication of their degree of certainty. Details of current trends that are likely to continue should also be given, for example:

- the increasing use of the internet;
- increasing storage of photographs and video files;
- the trend towards home working.

5 Implementing IT service management

Starting from the point of knowing whether a component such as a server is of high, medium or low usage, an assessment then needs to be made of the impact of any known business requirements that will affect it. For example, if the processor of a key server is already being heavily used and the plan is to increase the number of users then this would raise a red flag and lead to a recommendation to upgrade or replace the current server. Conversely, if a server has low utilization and there are no upcoming changes then it will probably suffice for another year. This information is probably best represented in a table. The analysis, albeit basic, will help to inform the decision-making process and provide more concrete evidence for IT expenditure than otherwise would be the case.

Your general analysis should also be supplemented by any sizing exercises carried out by the suppliers of technology that are to be implemented during the planning horizon. For example, many organizations considering virtualization will bring in an external company to conduct a detailed assessment of what will be required to consolidate the server farm, and this is valuable input into their capacity planning process. Such companies will often have access to more relevant (and more expensive) tools that they can use to your benefit. This can also be true of existing service providers who may allow you to use standard tools that can show your usage of their resources at the moment, such as web-based monitoring of wide area network links or internet connections. Any sources of capacity information that add to the overall picture should be welcomed and used to full effect.

To conclude the analogy we started this section with, a basic capacity management process such as we are suggesting here is equivalent to providing a car with a working fuel gauge even if it doesn't specify exactly how many litres are left in the tank. Just knowing whether you are a quarter or three quarters full is often enough information to allow sensible decisions to be made, without the time and expense of going to the next level of detail for little practical benefit.

Summary

- Capacity management is about understanding where you are now with your infrastructure, what is likely to happen over the next six to twelve months and then assessing the impact and planning for it, both technically and financially.
- Using capacity/network monitoring tools can be an inexpensive way of monitoring your capacity without making it an administrative nightmare.
- Talk to the business regularly about its future capacity needs and to understand its existing patterns of usage.

Service delivery processes

> - A Capacity Plan should be produced at least annually and should set out what needs to be put in place during the year to avoid service issues arising through lack of capacity.

Next steps

> 1. Identify your key service components and start to monitor their capacity.
> 2. Talk to the business about what it knows is going to happen in the next six to twelve months.
> 3. Create a Capacity Plan summarizing where you are now and where you expect to be in twelve months' time.

Information security management

Objective

To manage information security effectively within all service activities.

Never a day seems to go by without some form of security-related incident being reported in the media; from loss of data in transit through to orchestrated hacking attempts, it always makes good press and causes embarrassment to the individuals and organizations affected. It's one of the few areas of IT service management in which you have a legal responsibility to take action to protect the data you hold, particularly if it refers to identifiable individuals. The penalties for contravening the Data Protection Act in the UK have recently been strengthened and this is likely to be an increasing worldwide trend over the next few years.

So how do you reduce the likelihood of your organization falling victim?

The first thing to say about information security is that it is a business issue and that, whilst the IT function can do a lot to contribute towards the security of the organization's information, it cannot and should not be solely responsible for it. The reason for this is that there are many ways in which information security can be compromised that lie outside of the control of IT. Paper documents containing sensitive information can be lost or left out on desks by business staff, doors and windows can be left unlocked and employees can be overheard on the train discussing confidential cases or deals. It is everyone's responsibility and this needs to

5 Implementing IT service management

be emphasized to (and ideally by) the senior management of your organization if this hasn't been done already.

There is an international standard for information security called ISO/IEC 27001 that has been widely implemented by organizations that have a particular need to be, and be seen to be, secure. Often these are IT suppliers who wish to prove to their clients and prospects that they can be trusted with their data, but the range of organizations that are certified is growing over time as information security becomes more of an issue.

The ISO/IEC 27001 standard requires that an information security management system (ISMS) is put in place by senior business management and appropriately resourced. As well as ensuring that an appropriate policy is defined, this ISMS framework will monitor the effectiveness of the information security controls in place through an audit programme and concentrate on its improvement over time. We would recommend implementing (or at least working towards) the standard, but for those whose appetite for such things is limited we will set out in this section the main components you need to have in place to tighten up the information security within your organization.

Perform a risk assessment

The first step is to gain a good appreciation of where you are now with regard to the security of your information. This, of course, assumes you know where your information is in the first place – which is not always the case. Most organizations hold information electronically and on paper and obviously the focus within IT is almost exclusively on the electronic data stores. So you may need to do some digging to find out what information is held on paper and how sensitive it is. Once you've found as many sources as you can, make a list and call it 'information assets'. These may be databases, paper files, servers that hold the data, networks that transport it or the buildings that house it – anything that has a bearing on the way in which your data is held and processed.

Once you're clear about what information you hold, where and how, you can then start to perform an assessment of the risks to those information assets. Risk assessment has received a bad public press in recent years often because of its overzealous application in a health and safety context. The purpose of it here is to work out exactly where your organization's hard-earned money should be applied to maximize the benefit and address the most vulnerable areas. Otherwise you could end up spending money to tighten up an area that is already adequately protected, at the expense of another area that is a disaster waiting to happen.

Service delivery processes

The risk assessment is normally represented as quite a wide spreadsheet with a column for each item – see A.2 in Appendix A for an example. In information security terms there are three aspects of your information assets you will need to protect:

- *confidentiality* – preventing the wrong people from seeing it;
- *integrity* – that it remains correct and accurate;
- *availability* – that the right people can still get to it.

The risks to your information assets will depend upon your particular situation, but might include:

- theft;
- accidental destruction;
- accidental loss;
- virus infection;
- unauthorized access;
- corruption through hardware or software failure.

For an example risk assessment scheme, see the earlier section on IT service continuity as the principles are the same and it's often a good idea to cover these two areas as part of the same assessment to ensure consistency.

Having assessed the risks to your information assets, you then need to look at what can be done with the higher risks to reduce either the likelihood of it happening or the impact if it were to happen. This is the risk treatment and usually takes the form of introducing controls. Controls may take the form of revised working practices or could involve the use of relevant software such as an anti-virus program.

For those risks that can't be reduced to an acceptable level through the use of controls a number of other options are available to you, such as:

- avoid the risk, for example, by no longer holding the information at all;
- share the risk with someone else so that it effectively reduces your exposure;
- create a contingency plan to cope with the risk actually happening.

To complete the picture you then need to reassess the risks to see what effect your treatment will have; hopefully it will drop the risk level down a notch, for example, from high to medium or from medium to low. If it doesn't you may need to rethink your proposed actions to see if you can do more.

Things change over time so be prepared to go back to your risk assessment on a regular basis to check that it is still valid, adding new risks and updating existing ones where necessary.

5 Implementing IT service management

Controls

Information security controls lead on from your risk assessment and should relate directly to them. The controls could be:

- *procedural* – getting people to work in a different, more secure way;
- *technical* – for example, installing some software to detect and remove viruses;
- *physical* – for example, installing a better lock on the server room door.

Or any other kind you can think of that is appropriate to you. The point is that they are all about doing something about the risk. But they should also be appropriate to the level of risk that exists – too strict and you may stop people from being able to do their jobs; too weak and the risk may come to pass with disconcerting results. It's very much a balancing act and can lead to some difficult decisions. For example, how strong should you insist user passwords should be? You can enforce rules via the operating system or application – minimum length, special characters, numbers, repeating characters – the list of possible controls is quite long. But if you make it too hard to create an acceptable password you risk people writing them down and so compromising security even more. The number of password reset calls to your service desk may also rise giving you resourcing issues. If you are a bank or similar organization that has significant assets to protect then you will tend towards the stricter end of the spectrum. A manufacturing company, on the other hand, may decide that a lower (but not too low!) level would provide sufficient security to address the risk without causing too much upset.

It's always a good idea to make sure the controls are documented so that there is no doubt about how they should be working. They should also reference the risks they relate to so that everyone understands what their purpose is. An example might be a control procedure (and perhaps some software) to download and apply updates to server operating systems, the risk addressed being that of unauthorized access via someone hacking in from the internet using known security flaws.

Case in point

> Paper copies of confidential files were filling up the storage area so the IT Manager arranged for them to be scanned in and made available securely via the internet. Unfortunately generic logons were used and the password never changed so staff that left the organization several years ago still theoretically had access to the files.

Service delivery processes

There is no right number of controls you should have; the ISO/IEC 27001 standard goes into a high degree of detail about controls and lists a significant number of recommended ones. Unless you're intent on gaining certification to this standard this is almost certainly overkill, but it is worth having a look at them to see what good ideas you can glean from the list.

The information security policy

Working in conjunction with your risk assessment and resulting controls, the information security policy effectively sets out the 'dos and don'ts' that all of your organization's permanent and temporary employees, suppliers and third parties must follow. In this respect it is really a cross between a marketing document and a contract as its purpose is to inform and educate and also to act as a basis for disciplinary action if required. Because of this latter factor it is imperative that the policy is agreed by all relevant parts of the organization, including the board, human resources and, if appropriate, the unions.

Although we are referring here to the information security policy, it could in fact be a number of separate documents covering different areas. Often the approach taken is to have two policies:

- an acceptable use policy that applies to all users of IT systems and is required to be signed before access is given. This provides direction on internet and email use, removable media, software installation etc;
- an IT infrastructure security policy that sets out the policies of the IT department in areas such as virus control, access management and kit disposal.

Ideally both should be written in easily understood language, but this is particularly important for the acceptable use policy where the use of IT jargon should be avoided. Standard templates are available from the internet, but beware of adopting a policy that is too strict or too lax for your environment; often such template policies are written to comply with ISO/IEC 27001 and may specify a raft of controls that simply aren't justified within your organization. Adopting an information security policy that is unjustifiably stringent will mean that you will have your work cut out potentially over several years in order to bring your IT operation to a point where it complies fully with it, after all there's no point in having a policy if you don't follow it. You may be better to ratchet it down a few notches to a point where it is appropriate to you and then tighten it in a controlled fashion over time.

5 Implementing IT service management

Awareness and training

But there is no point in having a policy if no one knows about or understands it. Once the acceptable use policy is approved an awareness campaign should be mounted to get everyone to read it and to allow clarification questions to be asked. Even if all staff are required to sign to say they have read the document, it is likely that some still won't have actually done so and may still not comply with it. Articles in internal magazines, wall posters and the occasional email are all good ways of keeping information security somewhere near the front of everyone's minds.

Don't forget that the staff with responsibility for policing the policy may also need training either on the general principles or on specific software products, such as web monitoring or anti-virus products.

Security incidents

Unfortunately even the most stringent controls may not prevent security incidents from occurring, so you will need to be ready for them when they do. Part of the awareness campaign should be to encourage all staff to report any security incidents either to the IT service desk or via their line management. Such incidents could be:

- detection of a virus;
- theft of a password;
- loss of a memory stick;
- a hacking attempt from the internet.

Once reported, security incidents may have very particular requirements that set them apart from normal incidents. There are issues to do with the collection and preservation of evidence and the possible involvement of outside agencies such as the police. It is important to define how such incidents should be handled in advance and ensure that all IT staff are aware of the procedures (this would be one of your controls). You will need to try to balance the desire to close the incident once it is resolved against the need to keep it open in order to ensure that all the evidence possible has been collected. In order to do this, you may have to agree an SLA exception with the business and then omit some types of security incident from your regular statistics.

Monitoring and review

As with all of the processes of IT service management you need to keep an eye on information security and how well it is being addressed on an ongoing basis. Make sure it is on the agenda of regular IT management meetings and with the business, and review the key figures related to

Service delivery processes

security, such as the number of incidents reported, to identify any trends that are starting to form. It's also a good idea to carry out regular testing of your security provisions, either by yourself informally or, better still, using a third party. There are a significant number of companies who will probe your defences to try to identify ways in from the internet and many of them offer similar testing of the people-based controls too, such as obtaining access to the building or users' passwords. Fraud is often perpetrated from within an organization so bear this in mind when deciding how far to go with such tests.

Summary

- Information security is an increasingly important issue for all organizations, not only to prevent the loss of business assets such as customer lists but also to avoid falling foul of the UK Information Commissioner, who now has the power to impose fines for loss of personal data that was not sufficiently protected.
- It is a business issue and should not be completely delegated to the IT department. The ISO/IEC 27001 Information Security standard and its associated parts provide specific guidance on how to set up governance of security and detail many controls that could be used, if appropriate.
- A risk assessment will identify your areas of vulnerability and indicate the controls you need to put in place.
- An information security policy sets out your organization's approach to the issue and should be read and understood by all employees and third parties.
- Information security incidents will often require special handling and your procedures should allow for this.

Next steps

1. Put information security on the agenda of your next meeting with the business.
2. Start to create (with the participation of the business) a list of your information assets and assess the risks to them.
3. Draft an information security policy, get it agreed and then publicize it continuously.

5 Implementing IT service management

Design and transition of new or changed services

Objective

To ensure that new services and changes to services will be deliverable and manageable at the agreed cost and service quality.

So you've done all the hard work to define your services, negotiated an SLA with the customers, you monitor and plan your capacity, you have a clear idea of all your suppliers and the associated contracts etc. ... and then someone tells you that a project is starting to implement a new system.

Do you do what happens in many IT departments? i.e.:

1. Go to the project meetings.
2. Put the new servers in.
3. Wrestle with a few technical issues.
4. Go live.
5. Struggle to support it.

Or do you have a projects team that casually mentions on Friday afternoon that a new system is going live on Monday? After which it's your problem, of course; they have the next project to work on.

IT service management attempts to avoid all of this. It suggests you start planning early on in the project to incorporate the new service into the IT service management system. Any changes have to go through change control. Fortunately good practice (particularly the ISO/IEC 20000 IT service management standard) is fairly explicit in terms of what it wants to see, which means you can turn this list of requirements into a checklist for use during projects (see A.7 in Appendix A for an example).

The main culture change you will need to achieve is to do away with the generally held assumption that the IT department will support a new system at a moment's notice with no documentation or training, and regardless of whether the system actually works. You are the gatekeeper – no new systems or services go live unless you are happy that the prerequisites are met, namely:

1. *It has been agreed who will do and support what* – the responsibilities of the various parties in supporting the new system, including any target incident resolution times, should be documented and agreed in the SLA.
2. *You have a copy of the external support contracts* – if your service desk is to interact with a new supplier then you need to know the terms of that interaction. Get a copy then go over it in detail. Ensure

Design and transition of new or changed services

any support time frames are in line with the SLA; it's no good agreeing two days with the users if the supplier only provides a three-day turnaround.
3. *You have any new staff required in place* – if your existing team is already stretched then supporting a new system will be difficult. Try to ensure you get enough notice to allow time to recruit if necessary, and that the extra cost has been factored into the project.
4. *Your people have been trained* – it's difficult to support a system you know nothing about. Ensure there has been a skills transfer from the project team to your people and that they have attended any formal training courses that are available.
5. *The funds required for ongoing support have been agreed and allocated to your budget* – it is surprising how often a project proposal will completely miss out the ongoing support costs of a new system. Lobby to get them included so that you don't end up footing the bill from your existing budget.
6. *There is a clear definition of what success looks like* – ensure it's clear to all what the new service is supposed to achieve and appropriate metrics are in place to tell whether this has been the case.
7. *Everyone that needs to know about it, does* – have all the right people been involved in the project so far? Are there any other parties who might be affected by the new service when it's in live running and do they need to be consulted?
8. *The new system is incorporated into the IT service management quality system* – having gained some level of control over existing IT services, you don't want to lose it again when a new one comes along. The various documents and processes that you use to manage your services need to be updated to cater for the new addition. This may include the SLA, service catalogue, capacity plan, service continuity plan, configuration management database and service reports, amongst others.
9. *You are happy that it works* – this last point is particularly relevant and well worth spending some time on. Good practice proposes that you don't just take the project team's word that all the required processes and procedures work; they need to show you. You'll be surprised how often you hear the words 'oh, it's the first time it's done that!' during the acceptance testing and it will often take several iterations before the system has a clean bill of health. Obviously we're talking here about the parts of the system that the IT department will be handling – such as backups, creation of new users, running batch work etc. – not the actual functionality of the application (although it would be nice to have a warm feeling about that too).

Of course, it's much easier to meet the above criteria if they have been designed into the new system or service from the start. This is why as an IT manager you need to keep your ear to the ground and get in on any new projects at the earliest stage possible, whilst the requirements are

5 Implementing IT service management

still being defined. You will then have an opportunity to make sure that the service design criteria are addressed as well as the functional criteria before a solution is chosen. Otherwise you risk having to provide 24/7 availability using a single server and no out-of-hours support contract. Asking these questions at this stage may not make you popular, as the emphasis and enthusiasm is inevitably on what the new system should do as opposed to how it will be supported. But keep plugging away and ensure that service design criteria are included in any request for proposal that is sent out to prospective suppliers. This means that the cost of providing the required level of service should also be considered as part of the overall project cost, and this may affect the business case determining whether it happens at all. Again, this might not make you popular, but it's a truer reflection of the actual costs to the business, so it needs to be stated.

Summary

- This is one of the most important parts of IT service management because it cuts across all areas. If it's not done, the whole IT service management quality system becomes rapidly out of date.
- Ensure the delivery aspects of a new service are considered right at the start of the project and the costs are included in the initial business case.
- Plan your service acceptance testing early on – make it clear that acceptance is not guaranteed.

Next steps

1. Start to get the business thinking about the ongoing delivery of the service as well as the initial implementation.
2. Create a checklist of IT service management requirements and get it in use early on in a project.
3. Try to go back and fill in the gaps for existing services as much as possible.

6 The continual service improvement cycle

Continual improvement became a real focus for organizations in the mid-twentieth century following the Second World War. Organizations needed a way to take a controlled approach to making changes to their organizations or operating processes in order to make incremental improvements to efficiency and effectiveness. Many organizations are looking for the 'big-bang' approach to improvements, but it is important to understand that a succession or series of small planned increments of improvement is often preferable as this will not stress the infrastructure as much and will eventually amount to a large amount of improvement over time.

Many methodologies grew up around this desire for continual improvement; some faded away, others survived the test of time. Approaches such as Kaizen, TQM, Deming, Six Sigma and Lean all depend upon and build upon continual improvement and we'll have a brief look at them in this chapter, along with some suggestions of how you can get started.

Continual improvement in ISO/IEC 20000 – the Deming Cycle

The most widely known and often quoted model for continual improvement is the Deming Cycle, also known as the Shewhart Cycle or, more commonly, Plan-Do-Check-Act (PDCA).

This is the basic cycle upon which most other quality management approaches are based, including ISO 9001 and ISO/IEC 20000. The cycle is made up of four key stages followed by a period of consolidation to prevent backsliding.

- *Plan* – Establish goals for improvement. This can include performing a gap analysis and then planning the actions to be taken to close any gaps and achieve identified benefits.
- *Do* – Develop and implement the improvement in order to close the identified gaps.

6   The continual service improvement cycle

- *Check* – Compare the outcomes of the implementation against the measures of success defined during the planning stage to determine whether the action was a success and also whether the method was the best way to achieve it.
- *Act* – Once the planned actions have been reviewed for effectiveness and the outcomes reviewed for delivered benefits, a plan is put together that corrects any failings or inefficiencies. It may be decided that the remaining gaps should be left or that further work is required. This is all fed into the next round of improvement.

ISO/IEC 20000 fully subscribes to the Deming Cycle and requires that it be applied to all aspects including the processes, the management of IT service management and the management of the services themselves. A significant part of the standard is given over to defining how improvements should be captured, prioritized, managed and measured.

Continual improvement in ITIL

ITIL V3 devotes an entire book to the subject of Continual Service Improvement (CSI), which gives you an idea of how important it is considered to be. As well as the Deming Cycle, ITIL elaborates and identifies a CSI model (shown in Figure 11) for continual improvement and a strong linkage with the data and measurements that underpin each step.

The model asks a number of important common-sense questions to guide the user through the process:

- *What is the vision?* requires the examination of the business vision, mission, goals and objectives to ensure that any activities complement and enhance the organization's ability to meet its corporate aims.
- *Where are we now?* requires data and baseline information.
- *Where do we want to be?* is where IT and the business can set shared targets for this improvement or activity.
- *How do we get there?* seeks to lay out the method of implementation and draws from current service and process running and improvement activities.
- *Did we get there?* compares the baseline assessment (before) with a new, redefined current state (after) and seeks to establish whether the movement meets the targets set earlier.
- Finally, *How do we keep the momentum going?* looks at what could be changed or improved about the outcomes achieved and the method of achieving them, and suggests actions that could be fed into the next iteration.

ITIL then elaborates on this model with a 7-Step Improvement Process (although there is an argument that it's actually an 8-Step process

Six Sigma and continual improvement

because of the inclusion of the 'Identify vision, strategy, tactical goals and operational goals' step. The process draws an early distinction between what you should measure and what you can measure; it's worth considering what measures would be really useful (and in many cases meaningful to the business), even if you don't currently have the capability to capture the data effectively – this may develop with time, given the expressed desire.

ITIL indicates that, rather than this being a simple circular cycle, it is a knowledge spiral, by which is meant that certain stages rely on input from a lower level cycle – strategic improvements rely on input from tactical improvements that rely in turn on operational improvements.

Six Sigma and continual improvement

Six Sigma employs the DMAIC project methodology which loosely maps onto the PDCA cycle, as is shown in Figure 11.

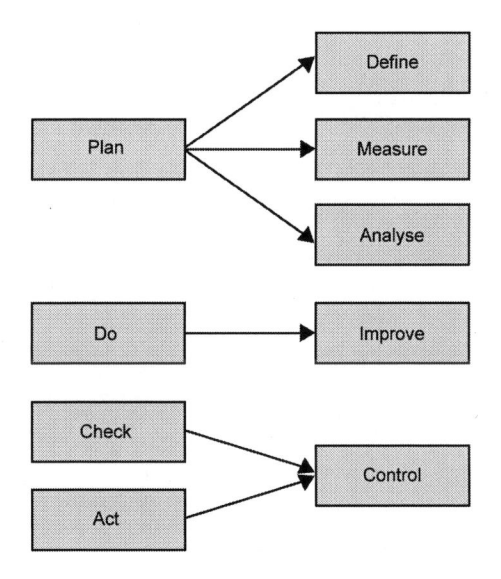

Figure 11 – Mapping of Deming Cycle onto Six Sigma DMAIC

For the immediate purposes of a small IT team the differences are probably too subtle to be useful, but Six Sigma may be a useful tool once your continual improvement culture is firmly established.

6 The continual service improvement cycle

Implementing continual improvement

You now have a flavour of how different frameworks and methods approach continual improvement. One of the traditional problems in this area is that many organizations have talked the talk but relatively few have truly embraced the concept. Instead, improvement is seen as a series of project implementations that are not reviewed and used as input to the next round of improvements. Continual improvement requires that actions are planned to determine the desired impact, implemented in a controlled fashion, reviewed for effectiveness in delivering the intended outcomes and this review is then used as part of the input for the next planning session.

But what simple steps can a small IT team take to start instilling such a continual service improvement culture?

The first is to encourage your team to identify improvements so that they can be captured and managed. These improvements could be large or small and cover any part of the IT service. This is similar to a suggestion scheme that operates in some organizations and you may decide to treat it as such, offering incentives or prizes if appropriate. You may like to add it to the agenda of regular team meetings. Log the improvement suggestions on a spreadsheet or database and then review each one to assess whether they are viable and beneficial. Define the objective of the improvement and how will we know when it has been achieved. Improvements that involve changes within the scope of change management should go through that process and a record of the change request number put against the improvement. Some IT teams categorize their improvements and report on how many have been achieved in each area.

Once this improvement management process is established, we can start to use it for improvements identified from other sources, such as:

- customer and user satisfaction surveys;
- suppliers;
- risk assessments;
- business relationship meetings;
- audit reports.

The key thing here is to try to establish a single place for the management of improvements so that an overall programme can be planned and an accurate picture maintained of progress and the benefits gained. Large scale improvements will be managed as projects and can be recorded as such on your spreadsheet. You may need to use categories such as large, medium and small to help manage the improvement list.

Implementing continual improvement

Summary

- Continual service improvement is a key feature of most of the current frameworks, methods and standards, all of which take broadly the same approach.
- The Deming Cycle consists of Plan–Do–Check–Act and forms the basis of most quality standards, including ISO 9001 and ISO/IEC 20000.
- ITIL defines a model and process that can guide you through the introduction of continual service improvement within your organization.

7 ISO/IEC 20000 – to certify or not to certify

This is an interesting question that we've been asked on many occasions ... 'Should we go for certification to the ISO/IEC 20000 standard or just implement those elements of good practice we find useful based on the available frameworks?'

To a large extent, this depends upon your organization's attitude towards certification. Some organizations see certification as a benefit in its own right; some see it purely as a box-ticking or money-making exercise. In this chapter we will look at the pros and cons of going for ISO/IEC 20000 from a small IT team's perspective.

But first let's tell you a bit about what would be involved in applying for certification and how you would give yourself the best chance of success.

The certification process

If your organization were to decide to go for certification to the ISO/IEC 20000 standard one of the first steps would be to select an appropriate audit organization. There is a list of approved options, but often this largely depends upon who the incumbent organization is for the auditing of other quality standards, such as ISO 9001 (Quality Management) and ISO 14001 (Environmental Management) if these are in place.

The audit process is in two stages. The first is likely to be a one-day visit to review progress to date and assess when it may be appropriate to return for Stage Two, final certification audit. Ideally you should not arrange the Stage One visit until the majority of your processes are in place. However, auditor views seem to vary on this – some regard the Stage One as an informal discussion to check that you're heading in the right direction; others treat it as a full-blown run through and expect almost everything to be implemented to the standard already. We would advise you to err on the side of caution.

The minimum time frame between Stage One and Stage Two is usually about three months as it takes this long to build up sufficient evidence in some of the new processes to show compliance. For a small IT team this

The certification process

will probably be a two-day visit, but we have seen a one-day audit and three days may be appropriate if your team is at the upper end of 'small'.

A few pointers from experience in making the audit visit as easy for the auditor as possible (and therefore giving you the best chance of first-time success):

1. Make sure you book an appropriate room (not too close to IT, but not too far away either) and arrange some form of lunch; supply as many drinks as he/she needs – auditors seem to drink a lot of coffee for some reason.
2. Create the (hopefully valid) impression of professionalism as the auditor enters the office – charts on the wall showing incidents logged and resolved, availability figures, etc. are a good idea.
3. Arrange for your manager/director to come over for a quick chat to the auditor to emphasize the level of management commitment to the process – physical presence conveys it all.
4. If possible, also bring in a customer to provide evidence of business buy-in – five minutes will suffice.
5. Ensure your relevant documentation is easily accessible – perhaps put it all on a memory stick (ideally encrypted so that it complies with your security policy) so that the auditor can browse it at leisure, or create a limited access logon to where it's stored online.
6. Hold a mock audit before the real one to practise conveying clearly your policies etc. – practice makes perfect.
7. Identify good solid examples of how your processes have been followed – for example, a specific incident that led to a problem that raised a change; check all the details are up to date and correct.

During the certification audit, the auditor will assess most areas of the standard and possibly identify any non-conformities against it. These are classified as major or minor. A major non-conformity would typically mean that further work needs to be done before certification can be granted and a re-audit will be required. A minor non-conformity is not usually a barrier to certification as long as the issues are addressed within a few weeks of the audit and a revisit may not be necessary.

If certification is successfully gained, the auditor will normally inform the organization on the day and the certificate is issued a few weeks later. Surveillance audits are then scheduled every 12 months until at the three-year point when a full audit is again carried out.

But you don't have to do it all at once; the ISO/IEC 20000 standard allows the scope of the certification to be defined by the following three parameters:

- location;
- organization;
- service.

6 The continual service improvement cycle

This means that certification to the standard could, for example, be awarded for 'all services provided to the London office', or 'the XYZ service to all business units at all sites', or 'all IT services provided to the manufacturing division'.

There are advantages to this approach in that the implementation can be phased, with the scope of the certification expanding in later years beyond the initial boundary. Even for small IT teams a limitation of scope is certainly an option worth considering.

Pros

Small IT teams may find ISO/IEC 20000 certification to be an effective tool for the introduction of good practice because:

- it provides a defined objective for the good practice project, rather than a succession of individual process implementations, and consequently may be achieved in a shorter time frame, with a very focused endpoint;
- it allows a 'wide and thin' approach to be followed to achieving the quick wins in each area – ISO/IEC 20000 is effectively a distillation of ITIL V3 into specific key points from which the most benefit may be obtained;
- it carries more weight both externally, with auditors and regulatory authorities, and internally with the board because it provides objective proof that the processes are implemented successfully;
- the auditors will return every 12 months, processes will stay implemented and not tend to fall into disuse;
- maintaining ISO/IEC 20000 certification adds weight to requests for assistance to other parts of the business – 'you must help us because this is needed for our certification';
- government agencies (certainly in the US) are starting to use ISO/IEC 20000 as a yardstick against which to measure the quality of their suppliers. This is projected to become more and more of a factor in the coming years;
- it could be a good unique selling point (USP) for your organization – or it can certainly allow you to compete on a level playing field against other organizations who are trying to use it as a USP.

Cons

But you do need to consider the following points before deciding whether or not to go for certification:

- 'Certificate on the Wall Syndrome' – caution should be exercised to ensure that everyone realizes that the objective of ITSM is not

ISO/IEC 20000 in itself; that is just a milestone, the certificate represents a step along the road to good practice, not the final destination. Don't forget that the original aim was to improve the quality and cost-effectiveness of the services delivered to the users and customers from the customer's perspective.
- It's probably not the cheapest option. You have to consider that all of the processes defined in the standard have to be performed and controlled to a certain minimum level of quality so you can't pick and choose which parts to do. This means that everyone in the team will need to be involved, so raising the resource requirements compared to a limited implementation of selected areas. Add to this the cost of internal and external auditors; although for a small IT team the actual certification audit may only be one or two days and the established audit bodies are still surprisingly reasonable in their daily rates (for the IT industry anyway).
- It's not easy. Setting up 16 to 20 processes to work in harmony in support of your services would be difficult enough if you could dedicate all of your time to it, but doing it whilst continuing your day job can seem like an insurmountable task. Our only reassurance is that putting the essentials in place will improve your day-to-day delivery so allowing more time to build and improve your IT service management system overall.
- Once you have it you either have to maintain it or face the ignominy of losing it (and the potential for bad press that it may bring).
- Going for ISO/IEC 20000 might not lend itself to a gradual implementation as the length of time involved might make the prize seem too far away.
- Even though it is the standard for ITSM, it only covers good practice to a certain depth. It sets out the minimum set of activities and documentation that an organization should have in place to demonstrate that it is in control of its IT services.
- Although it proves that you have achieved the level of compliance necessary to satisfy an RCB (Registered Certification Body), it does not certify that the services you deliver are necessarily of good quality or even the right ones, just that you are in control of them and have an active process for the monitoring and improvement of them.

6 The continual service improvement cycle

Summary

- ISO/IEC 20000 certification can provide a useful focus to your project and, once attained, may be an effective marketing USP as well as providing proof to internal stakeholders that IT services are managed effectively.
- Don't get too hung up on the certificate and recognize that it will take longer and cost more than a more limited implementation of good practice.
- Even if you come down on the side of not going for certification, ISO/IEC 20000 is a hugely useful tool for your IT service management improvement exercise because it can still give you guidance on what the minimum set of good practice should look like.

Next steps

1. Think about your goals in implementing IT service management.
2. Investigate how certification would be viewed within your organization and with your external customers.
3. Find out who you could use as external auditors and how much they would charge for input into your deliberations.

8 Tools

One of the things we have often heard said in relation to tools is that they don't matter; it's the process that's important. Whilst we agree with that to some extent, we also wonder whether the people who say that have spent days trying to shoehorn a new process into an existing tool that really doesn't want to work that way. What you end up with in this situation is a hybrid solution with lots of workarounds to make up for the tool's deficiencies or a different way of working, which is not an ideal situation. Of course, we would echo the general advice that prevails in the industry, which is that the ideal approach is to define your processes first and then choose the right system to fit them. Unfortunately, in a small IT team environment with a limited budget, this isn't always possible.

The right tool can enhance your ability to provide a good service immeasurably, but only if you invest the time in it yourself to understand fully how it works and how to configure it to suit your environment. This is an important point that could save you a significant amount of time and money; there is a temptation to blame an existing software tool for the fact that you aren't meeting your targets, but often the problem is a lack of training and time spent on set-up. Replacing the current system with a new one will not necessarily change that and if you're not careful you could end up in the same situation, but a good few thousand pounds lighter.

So think carefully before embarking on an IT service management software tool selection exercise and make sure you define clearly what you need and why the current system can't provide it.

Tools are available to help in a wide variety of areas and we have only attempted to summarize the main ones here. It is a fast-changing market and it would be wise to keep an eye on at least one source of information in this area, whether it's a website, a publication or an annual visit to an exhibition/conference. See the list of resources in Appendix B for some pointers.

Evaluating ITSM software tools

First, a few general points about the process of evaluating and purchasing tools to assist with your implementation of ITSM. It's tempting

8 Tools

to shortcut any kind of formal process and just go for some software that you or someone in your team has used before and knows to be good. Whilst we're not suggesting you spend a lot of time and money undertaking a lengthy tender process, we are suggesting that you should at least define your requirements first and use some objectivity in your decision process. There is a fair degree of hype prevailing in the software tools market and it's important that you give yourself the ability to focus on what really matters to your organization.

In basic terms, make a list of areas that need to be covered by the type of tool you are looking for and then define what it should be able to do in each of these areas. Assessing each one as 'must have' or 'nice to have' is a good idea too. As well as functionality criteria, don't forget those such as customer base, financial health and cost, to name but a few (see the next section for service desk software specifically). From research, probably on the internet, make a short list of 'possibles' and then rate them in each area, discarding any that don't meet all of your 'must haves' (hence you need to be sparing with your use of this rating).

It's fairly standard practice nowadays for software vendors to provide a download of their products for an evaluation period and this provides you with an opportunity to reach a considered decision based on hands-on experience rather than how it looks on the website. Don't forget to involve your team in the decision as they need to be on board with any new tool, and besides may know most about the area it addresses.

By following a basic but structured process you can have a higher degree of confidence that the tool you choose is the right one for you and you will be able to show your reasoning if questioned from above (or by an auditor).

Service desk tools

If you're lucky you will already have a tool that covers all the required areas and is all paid for, perhaps more by accident than by design. If you're not that lucky, then you will need to undertake a tool selection exercise. A word of time-saving advice on this – establish your maximum budget right at the start and then make price one of your first questions. Some systems are deliberately aimed at high-end customers and priced accordingly and you can rule out a fair number of options straight away simply because they are far too expensive for your needs.

Some of the questions you should ask and areas you should look at when evaluating alternative service desk tools for a small IT team are:

1. Does it cover the following IT service management areas:
   (a) incident management;

Service desk tools

  - (b) problem management;
  - (c) service level management;
  - (d) service reporting;
  - (e) change management;
  - (f) configuration management;
  - (g) other areas in which such tools may have functionality include service catalogue, release management, supplier management and purchasing – you need to decide whether these will be required or not.
2. Check for how long each process has been implemented – if it's recent then it's probably fairly basic. It's often the change and configuration modules that indicate the maturity of the tool.
3. Can the various records be linked within the system – for example, incidents to problems, problems to changes?
4. Understand what the development priorities are and how many people are working on delivering them – does the product have a future?
5. How good is it at integrating with other tools and systems – for example, directory services, an asset discovery tool and an event monitoring tool?
6. Is it web-based (accessed via a browser) or is there a client?
7. Is there a SaaS (Software as a Service) option? This can be cost-effective as long as you are comfortable with the potential security and availability issues.
8. What is the pricing structure? Make sure it's clear what the cost would be for all the required modules for the number of people you have in your IT team.
9. Are you eligible for educational or charity pricing? It's always worth asking if you fall into this category.
10. Is there a self-service interface for use by users?
11. Can it send emails at specific points in a process and how configurable are they?
12. Does the software architecture (operating system, database, reporting tools, etc.) fit in with your organization's IT strategy?
13. How much training and consultancy will be required? This can add significantly to the overall cost of the system.
14. Does it have a facility to create incident and request models – i.e. frequently used records that can be created quickly?

There are many other criteria you may decide to use based on your particular requirements and we don't attempt to list them all here; the point is that you have defined what you are looking for in advance and don't go purely by 'gut-feel'. Also be aware that this is a competitive market and suppliers will often be prepared to reduce their prices to close the business, so don't be afraid to negotiate. At least two reference visits are highly recommended, ideally to existing users of a similar size and industry to yours.

Configuration and release management tools

Configuration (or, often more correctly, 'asset') management tools have been around for many years and there is a wide variety of mature, functional systems to choose from. Generally, these will go out and automatically scan your network to find everything that has an IP address and, in some cases, peripherals too. This is usually achieved using a variety of methods including:

- Ping (UCMP protocol);
- SNMP (Simple Network Management Protocol);
- NetBIOS (often used to discover Windows-based devices).

Once found, the tool will attempt to collect as much information about the device as it can, often distributing a small piece of client software that will then report back more detail on hardware and software installed. This information is then collated via a management interface that allows different views and reports to be produced.

Such tools can be a godsend if they are implemented properly, integrated well and people know how to use them. The key thing is that you must be able to trust what they are telling you. If you can't then they're of limited value, so it's worth putting in some extra time to understand the mechanism the tool uses to collect its information and the potential issues that could arise to prevent it doing so (e.g. lack of admin access to a device or a firewall blocking the protocols it uses).

The ideal is to run the tool every few days and have the information automatically updated in the service desk tool so that you can link incidents, problems and changes to the configuration items. For this reason, the choice of configuration management tools is often limited to those with which the vendor of your service desk system supports interfaces.

Once it has been running for a while (maybe a few weeks), carry out a limited configuration verification audit to physically compare what the tool is telling you with the reality on the ground. If the two compare favourably then all is well; if not, some investigation is required to see if the issue is procedural or technical.

Higher end tools may venture further into the area of true configuration management rather than just asset management, allowing relationships between components such as servers, applications and services to be represented, sometimes graphically.

Event monitoring tools

Wouldn't it be nice to know when something has gone wrong in your infrastructure before your users tell you? This is one of the aims of the event monitoring tool. Using many of the same techniques as the configuration management tool, this type of software will alert you in a variety of ways (including email, pager, text message and visually) if a component of your infrastructure is no longer responding. It's then a relatively simple job to interface it with your service desk tool so that an incident is automatically raised. This is usually by sending an email to an inbox that is monitored by the service desk tool. Care needs to be taken that you don't end up with lots of 'junk' incidents being created as a result of the event monitoring tools being too sensitive, so a period of fine-tuning is normally required.

Components that can be monitored include servers, routers, switches, Uninterruptible Power Supplies, Storage Area Networks and sometimes even air conditioning units. It largely depends upon whether the component supports SNMP, so this is something else to consider when deciding between hardware alternatives. The range of possible items to monitor is also quite impressive as many of the tools can detect problems with email server queues, database table sizes and even run small programs you can create yourself to check on the health of anything important to you.

If you get the right one, event monitoring tools can be extremely useful. You may wish to buy one that allows you to create a visual map of your infrastructure, including servers, routers and switches and project it onto the wall or put it on a big screen that is visible from the service desk. This works wonders for working out straight away what has failed even before the user calls start coming in. It looks good when you show people round too.

Performance and capacity planning tools

Another area in which software tools can assist you in implementing effective IT service management processes is in performance and capacity monitoring. In many cases the tools that are bundled with the server operating system are perfectly adequate to track processor and disk usage on a regular basis, and often an event monitoring tool will also include the capability to record key measures of capacity and performance via SNMP.

The key here is to make the process as automated as possible so that human intervention is minimized. Most tools will be able to record

8   Tools

statistics to files, which can then be used to create graphs for analysis. This will save you an enormous amount of time over the labour-intensive alternative.

A few can then take the next step, which is to predict capacity based on recorded metrics – i.e. true capacity planning. This often comes at a price, however, and tends to remain more of an art than a science in making the required predictions of future system usage.

Information security management tools

In addition to the usual firewalls, internet monitoring and virus-scanning software, there are several types of tool that you may find useful in helping to secure an SME environment. These include:

- Intrusion detection systems – these help to spot unusual activity on your network that may indicate an external (or internal) attack. Still a little pricey for a small IT team but they are coming down in cost.
- Data loss prevention (DLP) – will monitor where your data is being saved or sent to according to your security policy. For example, they could detect credit card data being saved to a memory stick or customer lists being sent to an email address.
- Event log management – these tools have the ability to scan the event logs across all of your servers and identify unauthorized actions or access attempts, as well as providing effective log archiving in accordance with good practice.

Summary

- In a small IT team with limited resources the right software tool can be worth its weight in gold in automating key tasks and making the process of applying and running with good practice as painless as possible. The key here is to choose the right tools and implement them effectively, integrating where practical and beneficial.
- Ideally you should define your processes before choosing a new tool that is capable of implementing them.
- Our advice is usually to make the most of your existing tools before looking for something new; often a perceived lack of functionality turns out to be a lack of understanding and training.

Information security management tools

- Useful tools are available in a wide range of IT service management areas; look around but think carefully about how you will integrate them when shopping for a new one.

Next steps

1. Assess your existing IT service management toolset – does it have the functionality you're going to need?
2. Ask yourself whether you're really using your existing tools to their full capabilities – is training required?
3. Identify additional areas where tools may save you a lot of time if implemented early and start to define your requirements.

9 Case studies

Sandwell Homes

In June 2009 the ICT Services Unit at Sandwell Homes successfully achieved certification to ISO/IEC 20000, the International Standard for IT Service Management. Sandwell Homes provides social housing services to over 30,000 tenants and leaseholders in the Sandwell region of the West Midlands.

The IT team consisted of a total of 15 members of staff, including an IT Manager and two team leaders. Help desk, desktop support and infrastructure services were provided to 950 users spread across nearly 30 sites, although some services such as LAN and WAN (Wireless Area Network) support were outsourced to a third party. Applications were largely packaged with some web and database development being carried out in-house.

Over the preceding two years the ICT unit had attempted to implement aspects of ITIL, but with limited success. As a result, although incident management and financial management processes were reasonably well developed, no other aspects of good practice were yet in place. The service provided was variable with many issues caused by unco-ordinated changes and major incidents were almost a daily occurrence. Because of this the unit's overall reputation within the business was lower than desired, although most individuals were highly regarded.

9 Case studies

The ICT Manager decided to bring in a consultant to speed up the implementation of good practice and one with experience and focus on the needs of small IT teams was selected. Through a process of workshops and meetings, the management team at Sandwell Homes began the definition and implementation of the required policies and processes. Regular, minuted meetings were arranged within the small management team and with the rest of the department in order to communicate key points, discuss issues and inform staff of upcoming changes. The tools in use were evaluated for their degree of support for the new processes and new ones introduced where required. It was decided to keep the current service desk tool as it provided good support for the ITSM processes that had not yet been implemented, such as change and problem management. However, a new configuration management tool was introduced and a third party contracted to interface it with the service desk system.

Regular meetings were initiated with key stakeholders on the business side to discuss the current service and new requirements and to negotiate a Service Level Agreement. This resulted in the turnaround of a key site that previously had been highly critical of the IT service provided. A skills audit was followed by a comprehensive training plan covering good practice and soft skills in addition to technical knowledge, with the management and internal audit team attending the ISO/IEC 20000 Auditor course and passing the multiple-choice exam.

The 11-month project culminated in a two-day audit by an external auditor who certified Sandwell Homes to the standard without any non-conformities.

The achievement is all the more satisfying for the organization as it was carried out during a period of significant technical change, which included several large office moves, a migration from Novell to Microsoft infrastructure, a new email system and the installation of Voice over IP telephony.

9 Case studies

Accord Group

The Accord Group consists of six member companies, each with a separate Chief Executive and management structure. The IT team provides a corporate IT service to each of the companies covering around six hundred users across a wide variety of remote sites. Reporting to the Information Systems Manager are six members of staff, covering help desk, desktop and infrastructure support, applications support and training.

The IS Manager, who was ITIL V2 manager-qualified, had recently purchased a new service desk system that incorporated modules for incident, problem, change and configuration management, with an add-on for automated discovery of assets. This was implemented as part of a service improvement project, using the ISO/IEC 20000 standard as a guide. All staff attended the ITIL V3 Foundation course and took the exam to gain the qualification.

A set of template documents was used as the starting point for the IT service management quality system. The various policy, process and procedural documents were tailored to Accord's requirements and a filing structure set-up in Microsoft SharePoint to hold them. The incident management process was addressed first, along with request fulfilment, and a self-service interface was experimented with to ascertain how much detail could reasonably be obtained from users when logging incidents and requests.

Once the new system was live on incident and request management, a problem management process was followed fairly quickly by a change management process. After a couple of months, however, staff feedback was clear that the pace was too fast, given the day-to-day workload, and a period of consolidation was taken before relaunching the change management process once more.

On the service level management side the IS Manager, based on advice from the auditor, decided that an initial scope incorporating just one of the six member companies would be appropriate and an SLA was discussed and agreed with the Chief Executive of that organization. However, a presentation was delivered to all CEOs of the group, all of whom expressed interest in being involved in the IT service improvement project over a period of time.

9   Case studies

Various activities were engaged in to increase the profile of the IT team within the group, including individual 'My job in sixty seconds' presentations (which were delivered via desktop videoconferencing to showcase the technology), articles in the group magazine and an IT roadshow.

A risk assessment exercise was carried out across all main sites and a revised information security policy was created and approved by the board. The IT Service Continuity Plan was revisited and updated with a test plan and the disaster recovery contract checked for accuracy. After some evaluation a new software product was adopted to provide network, availability and capacity monitoring capability.

Despite being busy with the absorption of a new group member and the associated IT service take-on requirements, Accord Group achieved certification to ISO/IEC 20000 in 2011 after a project lasting around 14 months.

10 Additional processes and concepts relevant to IT service management

In this chapter we would like to make you aware of a few additional processes and describe some of the areas outlined in Chapter 2 in more detail.

Additional processes

There are several processes that are new to ITIL V3 but which don't yet exist in ISO/IEC 20000. These processes can deliver value to small IT teams but are often more complicated to implement, or to extract the value from them. We'll cover the essentials of the key processes here with a little detail about what value a small IT team might be able to derive from them and any issues and tips we feel are useful to be aware of. For a full appreciation of these processes we would strongly recommend reading the ITIL books and/or going on a course.

Service portfolio management

ITIL defines service portfolio management as 'a dynamic method for governing investments in service management across the enterprise and managing them for value'. This takes the service catalogue concept further and extends it at either end to include the management of those services that are anticipated, planned, in development, in transition, or in any stage of decommissioning or retirement. Service portfolio management is about joining up your service strategy with the processes involved with taking it from cradle to grave, and includes the pre-live activities of define, analyse, approve and charter.

For small IT teams, the concept is still a valid one, although a full blown process may not be necessary. Assess what services the organization needs you to be developing in order to deliver against its strategy and draw up a full service portfolio list.

Additional processes

Transition planning and support

Transition planning and support covers some of the aspects previously within the release management process (in ITIL V2) but provides considerably enhanced guidance. Its goal is to plan and co-ordinate the resources needed to ensure that new or significantly changed services are implemented appropriately so that they create the expected value.

Basically, transition planning and support is about managing service transition projects. This area is very well covered by project management frameworks such as PRINCE2 or PMBOK. ITIL V3 does not provide a detailed explanation of all aspects of project management but highlights the most important activities for managing service transition projects and assists in identifying interfaces with the other service management processes.

From a small IT team perspective, the guidance given is useful as a basic project management approach but, if the organization has an existing project management methodology, this should be used and perhaps bolstered by the guidance in this section.

Service validation and testing

Service validation and testing, like transition planning and support, is a process that, in some larger organizations, is dealt with as a matter of course as part of the management of the project to implement a release. The principal goal is to assure that a service is fit for purpose and fit for use and will provide the expected value to the customers and their business.

It does this by defining the desired service quality and level of acceptable risk, and by influencing the release and change policies to ensure that all releases and changes are subjected to a level of testing and validation appropriate to the organization's needs. The process tasks are not necessarily performed in sequence and can be undertaken in parallel, but include:

- validation and test management (planning, controlling and reporting of activities throughout the test process);
- plan and design tests;
- verify test plan and test design;
- prepare test environment;
- perform tests;
- evaluate exit criteria and report;
- test clean-up and closure.

A series of test models are created that define what is to be tested and how each element will be tested. These are standard models that can be

10 Additional processes and concepts relevant to IT service management

applied to each area of each service being assessed using different perspectives, levels of testing and approaches.

Whilst the full service validation and testing process is not mandatory for any organization, failing to adequately test changes and releases is by far the biggest cause of headaches. This hits smaller teams especially as they often do not have the necessary resources to divert to deal with a sudden influx of incidents caused by inadequately tested changes.

Knowledge management

Knowledge management seeks to help the organization improve the quality of information required for decision making by establishing a structured approach to the gathering, analysis, storage and dissemination of service knowledge and information across the organization. The underlying purpose is to improve efficiency by reducing the need to rediscover knowledge and ensure that the right information is available to the right person at the right time.

There is a hierarchy recognized in knowledge management that seeks to translate data into wisdom:

- *Data* – raw data about events or discrete facts that can be used as the building blocks for analysis.
- *Information* – contextualized data, meaning that the data has been analysed to derive meaning relevant to the organization or situation.
- *Knowledge* – a combination of information and experience, ideas, insights, values and judgements of individuals that give the information power and makes it relevant for decisionmaking.
- *Wisdom* – where knowledge becomes part of the awareness of the organization. The knowledge has become commonplace, aids judgement and is no longer restricted to individual instances. It is broadened into principles and the wider context of the organization.

The knowledge management process details a structure known as the SKMS (Service Knowledge Management System), which brings together the data held in repositories such as the CMDB and enhances it with other structured and unstructured data and information in order to give a range of views of the represented knowledge.

When setting up a knowledge management process, thought needs to be given to:

- how the process will be governed – process, roles and responsibilities, etc.;
- the transfer of knowledge around the organization and the security implications this may create;

- how data and information will be managed – what data and information is required, what is the information architecture and quality standards, what procedures will be put in place to manage the data and information.

In terms of a small IT team, this is a process that will grow rather than be implemented. Provided all the data and information being collected is being used in a controlled fashion, bringing it all together over time should be achievable. Much of the source data will be collected in repositories such as the CMDB, the Capacity Database, the Service Catalogue and other existing databases. Other pieces of the puzzle will require thought as to how to structure the SKMS such that experiences can be recorded and used and how the SKMS can be linked to external sources such as weather information or supplier systems.

Additional concepts

Capability Maturity Model Integration

The Capability Maturity Model Integration (CMMI) is based upon work originally done by the Carnegie Mellon University to create a model for assessing the software development processes of an organization against a stepped scale of 'maturity'. The CMMI model built upon the original CMM and widened the scope to allow organizations to assess their maturity for their services (establishment, management and delivery), their acquisition activities (for products and services) as well as the development of products and services.

The model defines five levels of maturity:

1. Initial (chaotic, ad hoc, individual heroics) – the starting point for use of a new process.
2. Managed – the process is managed in accordance with agreed metrics.
3. Defined – the process is defined and confirmed as a standard business process.
4. Quantitatively managed.
5. Optimizing – process management includes deliberate process to optimize and improve.

Used correctly, the CMMI can be very useful in giving an assessment of each process or of the organization as a whole and can be used to demonstrate gaps and progress, as shown in Figure 12.

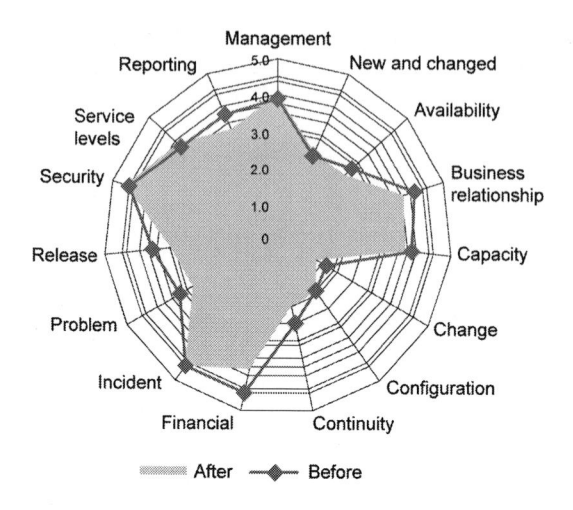

10 Additional processes and concepts relevant to IT service management

Figure 12 – CMMI gap analysis chart

ISO/IEC 27000

This is a family of international standards that provide a good practice solution to a range of regulatory and operational security issues faced by organizations. It provides guidance on areas such as security policy, organization, personnel security, communications and operations management, access control, system development and maintenance, business continuity management, physical and environmental security, and compliance.

The family is made up of several parts (more are being developed all the time), the principal of which are:

- ISO/IEC 27000 – vocabulary and definitions for the 27000 series;
- ISO/IEC 27001 – the requirements for an Information Security Management System; this is the standard against which organizations can be certified in the same way as for ISO/IEC 20000;
- ISO/IEC 27002 – the Code of Practice; this gives detailed guidance on the controls that should be in place to ensure a level of security for the technology and information assets of the organization appropriate to its needs. Each control should be assessed against the specific circumstances of the organization.

COBIT

This stands for 'Control Objectives for Information and related Technology' and is a model designed to address the control of the entire IT function. It was originally developed in 1994 by the research institute

Additional concepts

of the Information Systems Audit and Control Association (ISACA). It supports and assists management in the governance of IT by providing a comprehensive description of a series of control objectives for all IT processes and by providing a mechanism for monitoring, measuring and assessing the ongoing maturity of the processes.

It is broken up into four management domains, which are:

1. Plan and organize.
2. Deliver and support.
3. Acquire and implement.
4. Monitor and evaluate.

Each domain contains a number of processes, each of which describes a goal, the requirements of the process and the criteria against which achievement should be measured.

ISO/IEC 38500

This is an international standard describing a framework for the governance of the use of IT by an organization. This is subtly different from (but closely linked to) COBIT in that COBIT is a model for the governance of processes within IT whereas ISO/IEC 38500 is a model for how senior management (the board of directors or similar) should govern and set strategic direction for IT across the organization.

It details six guiding principles:

1. Establish clearly understood responsibilities for IT.
2. Plan IT to best support the organization.
3. Acquire IT validly.
4. Ensure that IT performs well, whenever required.
5. Ensure IT conforms with formal rules.
6. Ensure IT respects human factors.

ISO/IEC 38500 specifies that directors should establish methods to direct, monitor and evaluate the organization's use of IT against business pressures and needs.

Lean

Lean is described as a mindset, the core idea of which is to maximize customer value while minimizing waste. Lean simply means creating more value for customers with fewer resources. Within IT Lean has been a relatively recent entrant to the discussion although it has been around in other industries, particularly manufacturing, for some time.

10 Additional processes and concepts relevant to IT service management

The five-steps for the implementation of Lean are:

1. Specify value from the standpoint of the end customer by product family.
2. Identify all the steps in the value stream for each product family, eliminating whenever possible those steps that do not create value.
3. Make the value-creating steps occur in tight sequence so the product will flow smoothly toward the customer.
4. As flow is introduced, let customers pull value from the next upstream activity.
5. As value is specified, value streams are identified, wasted steps are removed and flow and pull are introduced, begin the process again and continue it until a state of perfection is reached in which perfect value is created with no waste.

Because of its origins within the Japanese company Toyota, there are various non-English language terms and concepts used throughout Lean – such as *muda* (meaning waste), *mura* (meaning unevenness), *poka-yoke* (errorproofing), *challenge* (having a long-term vision of the challenges one needs to face to realize one's ambition and having the spirit to face that challenge), *Kaizen* (the concept that 'Good enough' never is, no process can ever be thought perfect, so operations must be improved continuously, striving for innovation and evolution) and *Genchi Genbutsu* (going to the source to see the facts for oneself and make the right decisions, create consensus, and make sure goals are attained at the best possible speed) – all of which feed into the total mindset.

Six Sigma

Six Sigma was originally developed in the mid-1980s by Motorola, as a way to measure and reduce the amount of variation or inconsistency in a process. It provides a quantitative methodology for continual improvement and lowering costs by reducing the amount of variation in process outcomes to a level suitable for the given organization.

It uses a statistical approach to deliver information, which can be used to make fact-based decisions.

Six Sigma specifies a five-phase improvement cycle, known as DMAIC.

1. Define the problem, the voice of the customer and the project goals, specifically.
2. Measure key aspects of the current process and collect relevant data.
3. Analyse the data to investigate and verify cause-and-effect relationships. Determine what the relationships are, and attempt to ensure that all factors have been considered. Seek out root cause of the defect under investigation.

Additional concepts

4. Improve or optimize the current process based upon data analysis using techniques such as design of experiments, *poka–yoke* or mistake proofing, and standard work to create a new, future state process. Setup pilot runs to establish process capability.
5. Control the future state process to ensure that any deviations from target are corrected before they result in defects. Implement control systems such as statistical process control, production boards and visual workplaces, and continuously monitor the process.

Each phase has clear objectives, tasks and techniques. Many of the techniques are 'borrowed' from existing industry knowledge, others are more proprietary.

Appendix A   Templates

A.1   Gap analysis checklist

Ref.	BS ISO/IEC 20000-1:2005 Gap Analysis Questionnaire	Yes	Action	Owner
3	**Requirements for a management system**			
	Objective: To provide a management system, including policies and a framework to enable the effective management and implementation of all IT services.			
3.1	**Management reponsibility**			
1	Through leadership and actions, top/executive management shall provide evidence of its commitment to developing, implementing and improving its service management capability within the context of the organization's business and customers' requirements.	1		
	Management shall:			
2	a) establish the service management policy, objectives and plans;	1		
3	b) communicate the importance of meeting the service management objectives and the need for continual improvement;	1		
4	c) ensure that customer requirements are determined and are met with the aim of improving customer satisfaction;	1		
5	d) appoint a member of management responsible for the co-ordination and management of all services;	1		
6	e) determine and provide resources to plan, implement, monitor, review and improve service delivery and management, e.g. recruit appropriate staff, manage staff turnover;	1		
7	f) manage risks to the service management organization and services; and effectiveness.	1		
8	g) conduct reviews of service management, at planned intervals, to ensure continuing suitability, adequacy and effectiveness.	1		
3.2	**Documentation requirements**			
9	Service providers shall provide documents and records to ensure effective planning, operation and control of service management.	1		
	This shall include:			
10	a) documented service management policies and plans;	1		
11	b) documented service level agreements;	1		
12	c) documented processes and procedures required by this standard; and	1		
13	d) records required by this standard.	1		
14	Procedures and responsibilities shall be established for the creation, review, approval, maintenance, disposal and control of the various types of documents and records.	1		
3.3	**Competence, awareness and training**			
15	All service management roles and responsibilities shall be defined and maintained together with the competencies required to execute them effectively.	1		
16	Staff competencies and training needs shall be reviewed and managed to enable staff to perform their role effectively.	1		
17	Top management shall ensure that its employees are aware of the relevance and importance of their activities and how they contribute to the achievement of the service management objectives	1		
	Score for this section:	**17**		

A.2 Risk assessment

Ref.	Asset	Likelihood	Impact	Score	Classification	Assessment	Treatment	Post-treatment likelihood	Post-treatment impact	Post-treatment score	Post-treatment classification
1	Building	Flooding of building			HIGH						
2		Building destroyed by fire			MEDIUM						
3		Brief power failure			LOW						
4		Prolonged power failure									
5		Organized en masse theft of equipment such as PCs,									

A.2 Risk assessment

Ref.	Asset	Likelihood	Impact	Score	Classification	Assessment	Treatment	Post-treatment likelihood	Post-treatment impact	Post-treatment score	Post-treatment classification
		phones, servers									
6		Prolonged loss of access to building due to major event such as industrial action, terrorism or violent crime									
7		Aircraft impact									
8		Vehicle impact									

IT Service Management for Small IT Teams

Appendix A   Templates

Ref.	Asset	Likelihood	Impact	Score	Classification	Assessment	Treatment	Post-treatment likelihood	Post-treatment impact	Post-treatment score	Post-treatment classification
9	User PCs and printers	Individual theft of equipment									
10		Hardware failure of individual PC, phone or printer									
11	Server room	Localized fire destroys server room									
12		Brief power failure									
13		Localized flooding									

A.2 Risk assessment

Ref.	Asset	Likelihood	Impact	Score	Classification	Assessment	Treatment	Post-treatment likelihood	Post-treatment impact	Post-treatment score	Post-treatment classification
14		Theft or sabotage									
15		Vehicle impact									
16		Overheating due to air conditioning failure									

Appendix A   Templates

A.3 Supplier catalogue

Supplier	Third party	Contract manager	Description	Process interface	Service level	Written contract	Renewal date	Amount p.a. (ex VAT)	Meeting frequency	Main contacts	Comments

A.4 Service catalogue

Ref.	IT Service	Description	Status	Available to
ICT01	Service desk	Single point of contact service desk for all users across all IT services, for the logging of: • Incidents • Service requests • Non-Standard Changes • Advice and guidance • Any other IT-related issues	Live	All users
ICT02	IT procurement	The managed procurement of IT products and services including: • Obtaining pricing and availability for IT-related items • Ordering of items • Tracking of order progress • Handling of order delivery • (significant	Live	All users

Appendix A Templates

Ref.	IT Service	Description	Status	Available to
		purchases to be routed via the Purchasing Team)		
ICT03	IT equipment life cycle	The installation, moving, change and disposal of IT equipment, including: Desktop PCs Laptop PCs Printers Scanners Telephones	Live	All users
ICT04	Desktop software installation	Installation and configuration of desktop software on the Supported Software List (available on request)	Live	All users
ICT05	User account administration	Creation, amendment and deletion of network user accounts, including set-up of appropriate permissions	Live	All users
ICT06	Email	Provision of email facility to allow the sending of internal and external emails,	Live	All users

A.4 Service catalogue

Ref.	IT Service	Description	Status	Available to
		including virus scanning and content filtering		
ICT07	File and print	Provision of a file storage facility and centralized printer management	Live	All users
ICT08	Internet access	Provision of a facility for authorized users to access the internet in a manner compatible with the internet usage policy, including anti-virus and content checking	Live	All users
ICT09	Website	Provision of the website and associated maintenance	Live	Customers and third parties
ICT10	Intranet	Provision of the intranet and associated maintenance	Live	All users

Appendix A   Templates

A.5   Service improvement log

Ref.	Date raised	Source	Action required	IT service management area	Required by ISO 20000?	Priority	Owner	Progress including dates	Status (open/closed etc.)

A.6 Major Incident Report

[IT Department]

Major incident report

Major incident title:	
Major incident date:	
Service desk ref:	
Report author:	
Date of report:	

Chronology of the incident
When was the first related incident reported? When was the incident recognized as being a major incident? State the date and time of all significant events and actions taken. When was the incident resolved? When was the major incident record closed?
The impact of the incident
Which sites and or/applications were down? What business activities could not be carried out? Can the financial cost of the incident be estimated?
The underlying cause, if known
Do we know what happened and why? Was a problem record raised? If so, state service desk reference.
Recommendations to lessen the likelihood of the incident recurring
What can be done to avoid it happening again? Who needs to take what action? References of any change requests raised.
Lessons learned
What could we have done differently? What process improvements have been identified? Have they been added to the service improvement plan?

Appendix A Templates

A.7 Service introduction checklist

New or changed service:

Completed by:

Date:

Ref.	Item	Provision
1	**Timescales and expected outcomes**	
1.1	When will the new or changed service become live?	
1.2	How long is it expected to be operational for?	
1.3	What are the expected outcomes of the new or changed service?	
1.4	How can these be measured?	
2	**Roles and responsibilities**	
2.1	List and describe the roles and responsibilities for implementing, operating and maintaining the new or changed service, including activities to be performed by customers and third party suppliers	
3	**Budgets**	
3.1	What are the ongoing costs of the new or changed service?	
3.2	How will ongoing costs be financed?	
3.3	Have any required funds been approved by the budget holder?	
4	**Staff resources and training**	
4.1	How much staff time will be required to operate	

A.7 Service introduction checklist

Ref.	Item	Provision
	and maintain the new or changed service?	
4.2	How will this impact on existing workloads?	
4.3	What skills must they have?	
4.4	What training has been/will be provided?	
4.5	Is any recruitment required?	
5	**Documentation**	
5.1	Is procedural documentation available for the new or changed service?	
5.2	Has existing documentation been updated to take account of the new service?	
5.3	Have requests for change been raised and approved for all changes taking place as part of the new service implementation?	
6	**Processes, measures, methods and tools**	
6.1	What new/changed processes, measures, methods and tools will be used in connection with the new or changed service?	
6.2	Availability management (inc. backups and business continuity)	
6.3	Capacity management	
6.4	Security management	
6.5	Configuration management	
6.6	Release management	
6.7	Incident management	

Appendix A Templates

Ref.	Item	Provision
6.8	Problem management	
6.9	Financial management	
6.10	Business relationship management	
6.11	Supplier management	
7	**Technology changes**	
7.1	What technology (hardware, software, network, etc.) does the new or changed service use?	
7.2	Will each component be under maintenance?	
8	**Service levels**	
8.1	What service levels are proposed for the service?	
8.2	Are they achievable?	
8.3	What is the impact to the service of not meeting them?	
8.4	How will they be recorded and reported upon?	
8.5	Are they documented in an SLA?	
9	**Contracts**	
9.1	What contracts with third parties have been agreed?	
9.2	Have copies of any contracts been filed in the correct location?	
10	**Communication**	
10.1	What relevant parties need to be communicated with as part of the implementation?	
10.2	Who will be the main contacts once the service is operational?	

A.7 Service introduction checklist

Ref.	Item	Provision
10.3	How will communication to the relevant parties be achieved?	
11	**Service acceptance criteria**	
11.1	What acceptance criteria will be used for the service to enter live operation?	
11.2	Has an Operational Acceptance Test plan been created?	
11.3	Has testing taken place to the satisfaction of all parties?	

Appendix A   Templates

A.8 - IT Skills Questionnaire example

Name:	
Job title:	
Date completed	

Skill	Level
Business skills	
ITIL	0
Business analysis	0
Project management	0
Networking	
General networking	0
Network security	0
VOIP	0
Web filter	0
Spam filter	0
Hardware	
Hardware maintenance	0
Server hardware	0
Printers	0
PC hardware	0
Thin client hardware	0
Cabling	0
UPS	0
Mobile telephony/PDAs	0
Laptops	0
Desktop applications	
Anti-virus client	0
Desktop publishing	0
Office	0
Imaging	0
Server applications	
Email	0
Server operating system	0
Directory services	0
Anti-virus server	0
Backup	0
Business applications	
Intranet	0
Accounts	0
HR	0
CAD	0
Servicedesk	0
CRM	0
Development	
Database	0
Document server	0
SQL reports	0
C#/Java/VB.Net	0
Web – HTML/ASP/XML	0

Rating scheme summary	
Level	Summary
0	None
1	Low
2	Medium
3	High
4	Expert

Appendix B References and useful sources of information

You may find the following links useful in finding out more about IT service management.

Organization	Website	Description
IT Service Management Forum	www.itsmf.com	The itSMF is an independent and internationally recognized forum for IT service management professionals worldwide. It is a prominent player in the ongoing development and promotion of IT service management 'best practice', standards and qualifications.
British Standards Institution	www.bsigroup.com	Develops standards in a wide variety of areas including IT service management; represents the UK on the relevant ISO committees.
APM Group	www.apmg-international.com	APMG handles the qualification and certification schemes for ITIL and ISO/IEC 20000 in the UK and other countries.
Institute of Service Management	www.iosm.com	The ISM provides guidance and support to individuals throughout the IT service management community. It aims to ensure that requirements for professionalism and ethical conduct are maintained and developed in its members.
Service Desk Institute	www.sdi-europe.com	A non-ITIL focused membership organization

Appendix B   References and useful sources of information

Organization	Website	Description
		mainly for service desk professionals.
International Organization for Standardization	www.iso.org	The world's largest developer and publisher of international standards. ISO is a network of the national standards institutes of 160 countries, one member per country, with a Central Secretariat in Geneva, Switzerland, which co-ordinates the system.
International Electrotechnical Committee	www.iec.ch	The world's leading organization for the preparation and publication of international standards for all electrical, electronic and related technologies.
Office of Government Commerce	www.ogc.gov.uk	The owner of ITIL and a number of related methods such as PRINCE2.

If you found this book useful, you may also want to buy:

- **A Manager's Guide to Service Management**
  Jenny Dugmore and Shirley Lacy

This book is intended to meet the need for a generic, broadly based book on service management. It provides a basic introduction on how service management best practices and standards can help a service provider to deliver services that add value for customers at the right cost and risk. It describes service management concepts and the broader service management landscape. The aim of this 6th edition is to substantially re-focus the 5th edition to give a broader based picture of the most important service management best practices, how they relate and how they can (or cannot) be used together.

· A5 paperback · ISBN 978 0 580 72845 7 · 150pp · £48.00
· BSI order reference: BIP 0005
For more details see http://shop.bsigroup.com/ISO20000ManagersGuide

- **Guide to the new ISO/IEC 2000-1: The differences between the 2005 and 2011 editions**
  Lynda Cooper

The new edition of ISO/IEC 20000-1 is substantially changed from the original edition published in 2005. The changes will impact any organizations which are already certified to this standard, those who are working towards certification. It will also impact those who use the standard as guidance as well as auditors, trainers and consultants who use the standard for their customers. This book will explain why the changes have been made, what the changes are and how to move to the latest edition. It will also cover the relationship of the standard to other standards.

· A4 Paperback · ISBN 978 0 580 72850 1· 120pp · £36.00
· BSI order reference: BIP 0124
For more details see http://shop.bsigroup.com/ISO20000DifferencesGuide

- **Introduction to the ISO/IEC 20000 series: IT Service Management**
  Jenny Dugmore and Shirley Lacy

The book forms the definitive guide to the second edition of
ISO/IEC 20000-1. It provides easily understood advice on "what the requirements mean", 'how to do it" and "what evidence will be required", and will predominantly explain and expand on Part 1 of the standard. The book includes a road map to the second edition and how it fits in the bigger picture for best practices.

· A5 paperback · ISBN 978 0 580 72846 4 · 236pp · £48.00
· BSI order reference: BIP 0125
For more details see http://shop.bsigroup.com/ISO20000Introduction